Wisdom & Advice for the Graduate

ABOVE AND BEYOND

Making Your Life Count

BY JAY STRACK

WORD PUBLISHING
Dallas • London • Vancouver • Melbourne

Unless otherwise indicated, Scripture quotations are from The New King James Version. Copyright © 1979, 1980, 1982, Thomas Nelson, Inc., Publisher.

Lyrics from "Living Life Upside Down" by Karla Worley and Gary Driskell © 1992 WORD MUSIC (a division of Word, Inc.) All rights reserved. Used by permission.

Environmental facts in chapter 18 are from The Christian Life Commission of the Southern Baptist Convention. Used by permission.

Library of Congress Cataloging-in-Publication Data

Strack, Jay.
   Above and beyond : making your life count / Jay Strack.
     p. cm.
   ISBN 0-8499-1164-8
   1. Young adults—Conduct of life. 2. Young adults—Religious life. I. Title.
  BV4529.2.S77 1994
  248.8'3—dc20   94–4135
                                         CIP

4 5 6 7 8 9 BVG 9 8 7 6 5 4 3 2

Printed in the United States of America

Dedication

This book is dedicated to the three wonderful women
God has placed in my life. They motivate me to
attempt to soar ABOVE AND BEYOND.

To Christina
"a Gift of God to my life"

My scuba-diving partner and my rock-climbing
enthusiast. Your spirit and dedication will enable
you to scale great heights. I pray as you climb you
will remember Proverbs 3:5—"Trust in the LORD
with all your heart."

To Melissa
"a Blessing from the Lord"

With your smile, shining spirit, and inner strength, I
know you will mount up with wings like an eagle.
My prayer for you is Isaiah 40:31: "But those who
wait on LORD shall renew their strength. . ."

To Diane
"the Bride of my youth"

I was first attracted by your obvious outer beauty,
but it pales to your inner beauty. You are the heart of
our home and a constant encouragement. Space does
not permit what I would like to write about my
feelings toward you, so I refer to Proverbs 31:28—
"Her children rise up and call her blessed; Her
husband also, and he praises her."

TABLE OF CONTENTS

1

BACK TO THE FUTURE

Man, what an exciting concept! Imagine the possibilities of traveling back in time to arrange events to ensure your own happiness. Standing now at the threshold of the future, you may find yourself dizzy with celebration yet uneasy about the unknown looming before you. *USA Today* reports 84 percent of high school graduates say they are excited about being out of school, but 49 percent admit the prospect makes them very nervous. Balancing on the edge of "the real world," it is time to bridle your anxieties over the future and to make peace with your past.

In the popular trilogy of *Back to the Future* movies, Michael J. Fox stars as Marty McFly, a typical teenager accidentally transported back to 1955 in a plutonium-powered time machine invented by his mad scientist/inventor friend, Doc Brown. Marty learned the hard way that past decisions have tremendous impact on both the present and the future.

Bill and Ted's Excellent Adventure was another Hollywood adventure back in time. Two teens traveled through history in a phone booth intent on kidnapping "historical dudes." The idea was to gain the knowledge of the past and relate it to everyday life in the California suburbia of the nineties.

While the idea of time travel is fascinating, it is hardly new. When I was a kid, the cartoon characters Sherman and Mr. Peabody blew our little minds with time-machine adventures. History teachers often give us the assignment to write a paper on when and where we would like to have lived in ancient times.

Gaze into the crystal ball of tomorrow and join me on an investigation of the wisdom of the past. We'll gain valuable insights to surviving the present and to succeeding in the future. Fasten your seatbelts, raise the tray tables, and place your seat in the upright position as we travel back in time to the days of ancient history.

Ideas can have great consequences or benefits. The Bible reminds us "As [a man] thinks in his heart, so is he" (Prov. 23:7). Other graduates may have greater grade-point averages or SAT scores; they may have the face and body of a model or artistic talents. But by taking the time to dream and read inspirational books like this one, you will soar above and beyond the norm. Turn the mediocre of the majority into the majestic accomplishments of the mighty in spirit.

Today is the day to transform your aspirations into achievements!

> Life is a leaf of paper white,
> Whereon each one of us may write
> His word or two, and then comes night.
> Greatly begin! Though thou have time
> But for a line be that sublime—
> Not failure, but low aim is a crime.
> James Russell Lowell

Peering through the windows of opportunity into the future, one can see the need for every individual to PLAN, PREPARE, and PRAY. Two diverse landscapes will be visible through the window: positive and pessimistic. The choice of views is yours.

PLAN FOR THE FUTURE

There is a tendency after graduation to let your destiny "blow in the wind." It's the "whatever happens next happens" syndrome. Don't be fooled into thinking your only requirement is to find a good job. Success doesn't occur through spontaneous combustion. Excellence is a by-product of hard work. I like Paul Meyer's recipe (from Success Motivation Institute) for a plan: "Crystallize your goals. Make a plan for achieving them and set yourself a deadline. Then, with supreme confidence, determination and disregard for obstacles and other people's criticisms, carry out your plan."

Vulnerability or victory is decided by a plan and the follow-through of it. Because you are unique, your plan must be specific to your life situation. Generic planning usually fails because it's someone else's plan. It's a good starting place, but it won't help you finish. Take the time to develop a sure route, a definite pathway. Comedian Lily Tomlin told a reporter, "I always wanted to be somebody, but I guess I should have been more specific."

One historic example of an urgent, yet well-thought-out, plan is found in the story of the Pilgrims' first American winter. The arduous voyage across the ocean finally ended on December 11, 1620, and many who survived were ill. The winter was mild, but the first months were grim for the inexperienced colonists, half of whom died by April 1621. Friendly Indians taught the settlers to catch fish and plant corn. They encouraged the Pilgrims to plan ahead with their seed corn and to work toward a harvest. At the time, eating the corn in their hands seemed like the best plan for avoiding famine and death.

Instead they looked toward the future and planted the seed corn. The harvest was good and in the autumn the Pilgrims observed the first Thanksgiving with the Indians as their honored guests. A poignant illustration that shortcuts do not bring lasting success, don't you think? What you have now in your hand must be invested, cultivated, and eventually harvested into a lasting bounty. These youthful years are your seed corn for the future; don't waste them.

PREPARATION FOR THE FUTURE

Having now devised a sure plan, move on to the next step. "Prepare?" you ask. "I've spent my whole life so far preparing. I am ready to *do* something on my own." *Prepare* is from the Latin *paro* meaning "to make complete, to point in the right direction, and to equip for battle." These are vital steps to healthy success. Allow me to further clarify the act of preparing as an infinite process of life. Its ingredients include learning, growing, and sharing. After all, the term *commencement ceremony* literally means "beginning ceremony." The emphasis on exams and graduation date looks toward the completion of a phase of life, but the commencement symbolizes the celebration of new beginnings.

In one graduation address Newton D. Baker made this profound statement: "The man who graduates today and stops learning tomorrow is uneducated the day after."

I often quote my friend, author Dr. Tim LaHaye: "The individual who fails to plan for the electrifying changes that will appear in the immediate future may be in danger of becoming unemployable." The key to holding a job in the future will be a good basic education inclusive of math and computers, continuing progress in education, and a willingness to work hard and serve people. Today the question is not usually whether to go to college, but how long and what major or field of studies.

USA Today: Tracking Tomorrow's Trends Today offered the following information:

- Around 92 percent of the members of the U.S. Congress are college graduates.

- Around 79 percent of the founders of the fastest-growing companies in the United States are college graduates.

- Around 97 percent of the country's corporate CEOs have attended college.

Just in case you're thinking in terms of sports, read what college president Theodore M. Hasburgh told his athletes: "A decade after graduation, almost everyone will have forgotten where and what you played. But every time you speak, everyone will know whether or not you are educated."

Although formal education plays an important role in your future, it is not the only type of preparation. In fact, there will be some for whom college is not possible or plausible. However, it is imperative that you view yourself as a winner. The spirit of "above and beyond" will serve you well in whatever job you have. Dennis Waitley, author and speaker, gives this definition of success: "It is not what you get that makes you successful; it is what you are *continuing* to do with what you've got."

Two attitudes of successful people can be true of you: "Whatever your hand finds to do, do it with your might" (Eccles. 9:10a) and "Whatever you do in word or deed, do all in the name of the Lord Jesus, giving thanks to God the Father through Him" (Col. 3:17). These verses present the wisdom of heaven for everyday life. Whatever your position, blue-collar, white-collar, or no-collar, may it be said of you as it was of the ancient Roman soldiers when they performed their duties in an above-average manner. Paid in salt, a precious commodity of the day, they were said to be "worthy of their salt."

Education is not found only in the classroom. In fact, much of the practical need-to-know information is attained as you live each day. Keep your eyes open, your ears attentive, your mind ready to absorb information from television, newspapers and magazines, radio, leisure reading, and the people you associate with daily. Take advantage of *good* talk radio and motivational or educational tapes in the car or while working out. The world offers you a university without walls, limited only by your environment.

For that reason, the selection of friends, what you listen to, the type of places you go to, all make up the environment of influence for life.

PRAY BEFORE, DURING, AND AFTER

Although I list prayer last, it is essential to bathe all plans and preparation in prayer. It is last only because it has no stationary position; prayer must permeate our every breath and move. It is indispensable in keeping values on track and goals focused. In fact, it is the greatest resource of power and inspiration ever to be made available to mankind. Nuclear power pales in comparison! Prayer holds the key to knowing God and to an ongoing relationship with Him.

Often a seminary student will ask, "How much do you pray every day?" For me, prayer is a constant process as natural to me as the air I breathe. I cannot imagine not communing with my Creator and Savior all through the day in addition to time set aside for devotions. Go back to the days when Christ walked the earth, leaving us an example for the future of how to live and how to pray. An intimate glance into His prayer life is given to us throughout the Gospels. He prayed:

- *The prayer of fear and surrender to faith:* "He went a little farther and fell on His face, and prayed, saying 'O My Father, if it is possible, let this cup pass from Me; nevertheless, not as I will, but as You will'" (Matt. 26:39).

- *The prayer of persistence in times of need:* "Ask, and it will be given to you; seek, and you will find; knock, and it will be opened to you." This is literally translated "keep on asking, keep on seeking, keep on knocking" (Matt. 7:7).

- *The prayer of gratitude for what God has done and who He is in our lives:* "Father, I thank You that You have heard me. And I know that You always hear me" (John 11:41b–42a).

- *The prayer of an intimate relationship:* "But you, when you pray, go into your room, and when you have shut your door, pray to your Father who is in the secret place; and your Father who sees in secret will reward you openly" (Matt. 6:6).

- *The prayer of faith:* "Therefore I say to you, whatever things you ask when you pray, believe that you receive them, and you will have them" (Mark 11:24).

Christ showed us that prayer must be *persistent* (Luke 11:8); bold (Heb. 4:16); in faith (Mark 11:24); *specific* (Luke 11:11); and *in Jesus' name* (John 16:23–24).

In the demanding days ahead, you will often be tempted to say, "I just don't have time today for prayer and devotions." Don't be fooled. This time with God will greatly multiply your effectiveness all through the day and affect the results of all you attempt to do. Prayer is not an option for the Christian; it is as essential as oxygen. I am a great lover of the sea. Some of my fondest memories are of the graceful dolphins dancing through the ocean. They must come up for air—they have no choice. I am reminded that I must "come up" for prayer; I have no choice if I am to continually strive for excellence in virtue and accomplishment.

Prayer is not our task; it is our privilege. Establish a time of the day for prayer, preferably before you start the day, while your thoughts are clear and free from distraction. Prayer is communication with God in much the same way you communicate daily with friends and family. Even though God knows your heart and your future, you cannot ignore Him, or your relationship with Him will diminish. "I will bless the LORD at all times; His praise shall continually be in my mouth" (Ps. 34:1).

The acrostic ACTS as pertaining to prayer has been used for many years. Try this simple outline:

A is for **adoration.** God is worthy of our praise and we should begin each day with adoration of His greatness, love, forgiveness, faithfulness, and holiness. God has many attributes worthy of praise. Use Psalm 138 to get started.

C is for **confession.** Though Christ has completely forgiven every sin in both our past and future by His death on the cross, we still must ask His forgiveness in order to keep our relationship growing in love. Confession is more than saying, "I admit it; I'm sorry." It is to agree with God about that particular sin, and to ask God to help you feel as much hatred for sin as He Himself does. Then and only then can you forsake the sin that holds you. Look at Psalm 51.

T is for **thanksgiving.** This is the part of your prayer time in which you can thank God for all He has given you, for the answers to prayer you have received, for the many blessings, and for all you are learning. A grateful heart is one that is blessed abundantly again and again. Psalm 103 is helpful in this area.

S is for **supplication.** Supplication is the act of requesting. There are many types of requests. Of course you will want to ask for physical and material needs, but above all there is need for spiritual power, and there must also be prayer for the unsaved or carnal Christian. Pray for and claim by name the salvation of those you are concerned about. Use Psalm 5.

TODAY IS YOUR OPPORTUNITY TO BEGIN TO SHAPE THE FUTURE.

As intriguing as the fantasy of time travel is, don't allow the daydreaming to deter you from reality. Every decision you make today will affect your tomorrow. No one ever plans to fail. They simply fail to plan. My favorite definition of insanity is: "to continue to do the same old thing in the same old way and somehow expect different results."

You cannot go back and undo poor choices. During the last presidential debate, both Dan Quayle and Bill Clinton were subjected to intense scrutinizing of their past. Various questions concerning decisions in young adulthood were repeatedly fired off from one city to the next. Both, in essence, gave the same reply: "I never dreamed I would be sitting in this chair in 1993 answering questions about my conduct while in college twenty-some years ago." There it is! As Gloria Esteban sings, "We seal our fate by the choices we make."

Robert Louis Stevenson predicted, "We must eventually all sit down at the banquet table of our own consequences." We anticipate our future achievements while others assess our past performances. Here are some suggestions about looking into the future:

- Do not choose to lose.

- Do not take your clue from the crowd.

- Do not be detoured by discouragement.

- Do not settle for the ordinary when the extraordinary is so close.

- Do not settle for surviving when you can succeed.

- Do not settle for natural when you can experience the supernatural.

- Do not settle for mere fascination with the future.

What you desire for your future can come true if you PLAN, PREPARE, and PRAY. In the words of Doc Brown, "The future is a clean slate." What you write on it today will be inspiration for the script for tomorrow.

The purpose of the study of history is to provide us the experience we need to navigate through the uncertainties of the future. In the next chapters, we will climb back into our time machine and experience firsthand three of history's greatest adventures.

2

CROSSING YOUR RUBICON

JANUARY 10, 49 B.C.—*The marching of soldiers sounds like distant thunder against the backdrop of the peaceful Rubicon River. From the boundary of the Province of Gaul, Caesar now leads his troops across the little river Rubicon. By his very presence he has committed the first act of war. This decision is not a flighty one. If you listen carefully, you can hear him cry out as he leads the troops across the waters—"The die is cast!"*

All of Rome fears Caesar as the civil war rages for three years. The Jewish historian Josephus, who lived through a Roman siege, wrote in The Wars of the Jews: *"The Roman warriors fought as if their weapons were permanently attached to them." When the dust settles, Pompei is defeated by Caesar and his elite fighting forces. He emerges from the battle as ruler of the Roman world. As Caesar crossed the Rubicon, he crossed over into a daring new role in life.*

Crossing the Rubicon" has become a popular phrase used to describe a definite step of commitment to a given course of action.

The Dictionary of Cultural Literacy defines the expression as "a dangerous, decisive, and irreversible step toward an absolute commitment to a planned endeavor." This move is an irrevocable one. It sounds very serious, doesn't it?

No matter how enjoyable or personally fulfilling your high school experience has been, it is now time to march forward. Walking across the stage to receive your diploma marks the beginning of a new life, and there is literally no turning back. You have crossed your personal Rubicon.

Stepping across the stage at graduation will not give you reign over the world, but it symbolizes your decision to move toward a successful future. A myriad of opportunities awaits you just on the other side. You can conquer the lands of tomorrow through DESIRE, DIRECTION, DETAIL, AND DEDICATION.

DESIRE

The word *desire* comes from the Hebrew *chamad*, meaning savory. You may have heard the idiom, "I want it so badly I can taste it." The psalmist David offered this meaning in Psalm 34:8 when he wrote, "Oh, taste and see that the LORD is good." His invitation to explore the goodness of God gave a guarantee of wanting more.

In sports the intense desire of the athlete to win is often defined as a "hunger." College football coach and sports broadcaster Ara Parseghian offers this view: "I use the word *hungry* to describe what I mean when I talk about desire. Being hungry provides you with the physical and mental energies necessary for success. The sacrifices that are necessary become easier when one places a goal or objective at a high level."

Successful, innovative people have always been fueled by a potent desire to achieve. I believe a wealth of talent lies untapped in our generation because of a lack of desire for success. Perhaps this talent awaits self-discovery in you.

Pure, intense desire motivated inventor Thomas Edison to continue trying after thousands of failed experiments. The invention of the light bulb alone required four thousand attempts. His life motto was "Show me a thoroughly satisfied man, and I will show you a failure." He often spoke and penned the words "Keep at it!"

Almost five hundred years later, the creed of Italian painter and sculptor Michelangelo is displayed throughout his works: "I hope that I may always desire more than I can accomplish." Only such a passion from the heart could have created such beauty.

How earnestly you are willing to work, plan and use your talents depends on how badly you want to win or succeed in your dreams. Pure desire permeates both the conscious and the unconscious. A hunger for excellence searches out new means of achievement toward a mark. Keep stretching, keep dreaming.

> *Send the harmony of a great desire vibrating through every fiber of your being. Find a task that will call forth your faith, your courage, your perseverance, and your spirit of sacrifice. Keep your hands and your soul clean, and your conquering current will flow freely.*
>
> Thomas Dreier, American author

DESIRE is essential as the launching pad to your goal.

To this first component, we must add DIRECTION. DESIRE without DIRECTION is merely a dream.

DIRECTION

OK. You are hungry for the goal. The desire is burning in your heart. You have *crossed over*. The next logical question is,

"Where do I go from here?" It has been said, "The world stands aside to let anyone pass who knows where he is going."

DIRECTION affords you a clear sense of objectives and specifics on the highway to "making it happen." The road map of life will offer you many detours and highways under construction. With a clear destination in mind, you will be less likely to be blocked by obstacles and difficulties. Goals serve as a focal point to the prize ahead and encourage you to strive for personal excellence.

Twin brothers Dorian and Derrick Malloy are living proof of overcoming obstacles by focusing on the future. When the teens started working at a McDonald's in a rough, tough section of New York in 1972, they might have looked like any other students to a passing customer. Those who worked with them, however, knew differently.

While disillusioned crew members tried to beat the system by offering free food to friends or by giving a minimum of energy to the job, the Malloy twins were giving their all to doing the job well. The two worked their way up from mopping floors to cooking and dressing burgers. "Our parents raised us to be honest, hardworking, and to be the best in whatever we might do," reports Derrick. This good advice soon landed the boys in a management-training program.

In 1985, the twins bought a nearby Wendy's unit with $50,000 of their savings (earned by working at McDonald's, mind you), $50,000 from a friend, and Wendy's financing. Today, the thirty-something brothers are grossing $2.5 million from their two Wendy's outlets and have plans for expansion of their territory. Sounds almost like a fairy tale, doesn't it?

As one who has placed faith and trust in the Lord Jesus, you can be assured of a wonderful future. True, the alleys and detours come as a surprise. Yes, there are delays and wrong turns ahead, but you can be secure in promises of the Word of God.

As we pray for guidance, we have the sure Word of the Lord to rely on. What better source of leadership than the God who sees tomorrow as we see yesterday?

> *Being confident of this very thing, that He*
> *who has begun a good work in you will complete*
> *it until the day of Jesus Christ.*
>
> Philippians 1:6
>
> *I will instruct you and teach you in the way you*
> *should go; I will guide you with My eye.*
>
> Psalm 32:8

DESIRE and DIRECTION are now our faithful companions, and it is at this time we must turn our thoughts to DETAIL. If we are to achieve great things, we must first give our attention to the smaller building blocks.

DETAIL

DETAIL is the secret to ordering your private world. Have you ever devised a seemingly perfect solution to a dilemma only to suddenly discover that one small detail destroyed your entire theory? The familiar cliché "Details, details, details!" may come to mind! In reality, we see that a tiny part can affect all efforts toward the big picture.

This is most evident in the world of art. In almost every country I travel to, I make it a point to visit the area where local artists display their talents. Strolling along the lanes, I notice that although the subject of the scenery may be identical, the paintings are not. Why? Simply because of attention to detail stressed by one and not another.

God cannot and will not take you on to greater things until you have proven steadfast and faithful in what has already been entrusted to you. Jesus illustrated this in the parable of the nobleman in Luke 19:12–23. In verse 16, the servant presents his master with the results of his work and investment. Having been given one mere *mina* to start, he now has earned ten as the result of careful planning. The reply of the master gives us a clear vision of how important the Lord views even our small beginnings:

> *Well done, good servant; because you were faithful*
> *in a very little, have authority over ten cities.*
>
> Luke 19:17

The message is evident: Our faithfulness will be blessed in a big way regardless of how small the start.

Having now DESIRE, DIRECTION, and attention to DETAIL, we must finish what we started by sheer DEDICATION.

DEDICATION

DEDICATION involves commitment to quality and performance, and often holds the key to turning a mere promise into surefire reality. It consists of consistency in intention and attitude, the power to change unfavorable circumstances, and the decision to triumph over pessimism.

Eliminate the words "I don't have time" from your vocabulary. Replace them with the statement: "I have not yet *made* the time."

The privilege of knowing future Hall of Famer and all-star catcher Gary Carter has been mine for several years. When I asked him how he got his start, this is what he told me: "I was determined to get to the major leagues in three years. If it took hustle and putting out more to get there, then that's what I was going to do." I took particular pleasure in reading this quote because I have watched his dedication as a player through the years.

I remember standing on the infield of Shea Stadium with Gary and my friend and pastor, Dr. Jack Graham, as we discussed the rehabilitation of his injured knee. Obviously, as a catcher, this type of injury is a great liability. Gary told us of the decision he made after surgery. His goal was to play well enough to help his team, the Mets, in the end-of-the-season pennant battle. This meant submitting himself to excruciating physical therapy in order to speed up the healing process, but Gary felt it was worth the pain. At that time in his life, Gary Carter had a valid excuse to feel sorry for himself. No one would have denied him time to lie about. He would have received a paycheck while he recuperated without risk or added pain. But for Gary, there was never any question. His dedication to the team and his own personal goals fueled his inspiration to endure. The knee healed in time, and Gary Carter stood up to bat for another pennant.

DESIRE, DIRECTION, DETAIL, and DEDICATION are your soldiers marching alongside as you face the new lands ahead. No doubt you have big dreams and plans. Now you must join Julius Caesar in the cry of decision: _"The die is cast!"_ Your irreversible act is only the beginning of exciting endeavors and adventures, otherwise known as . . . LIFE.

3

BRAVE NEW WORLD

Shh! We're hiding out here on the deck of the Santa Maria *to learn firsthand what the journey to the discovery of a new world is like. Smell that salt air, feel the spray across your face, gently sway with the rocking of the ship—oh, oh, I forgot my Dramamine! There is our leader, Christopher Columbus, staring pensively at the sea as though he expects land to rise up from the center of it. This has all he promised of an adventure extraordinaire!*

A study of his biographies reveals the combination of faith and will power that gave Christopher Columbus his drive. Think of the most difficult or fearful undertaking you have ever been faced with and then compare it to his. NO map of his destination other than the stars his hopes were pinned to. NO promise of success other than faith in His God and himself. NO encouragement from his crew except for one first mate who spurred him on. NO promise of wind for his sails but the wind of the Holy Spirit that "blows where it wills."

His leadership abilities are put to the test daily as an unbelieving, fainthearted crew mumbles in complaint. After a month at sea of alternating weather, they found that the food was about to run out. They had no faith in themselves—how could they possibly believe in Columbus? Yet he stood fast, impressing them with his ability to navigate by the stars. He seemed so sure of himself and his destination, but how so? He was headed where no man had ever gone before (James T. Kirk later navigated the S.S. *Enterprise* the same way).

From this man we can glean the benefits of PRODUCTIVITY, PERSISTENCE, and PIETY.

PRODUCTIVITY

In order to gain PRODUCTIVITY in his aspirations toward exploration, Columbus took up the study of mapmaking while he was yet a teen. Based upon the knowledge of the day, he formulated new navigational routes of his own. The young lad focused on the necessary education to achieve his goals. In Genoa, Italy, the place of his birth, a statue of Christopher's likeness was sculpted of him as a young man gazing out into what we can easily assume is a sea. Interesting, isn't it, that they chose his hopeful years to sculpt rather than the year of his grand discovery? I believe it was the look of innocent, hopeful longing that the artist wanted to portray. Therein was found the secret behind the productivity that Columbus built upon.

> *What we visualize and work for today*
> *ensures our tomorrow.*

Even though each day is a new, uncharted area for us, we have a map provided for us by the One who knows the seas because He made them. Now that's what they call having an *inside* source!

Lord, You are God, who made heaven and earth and the sea, and all that is in them.

Acts 4:24

Christopher Columbus had a hunch that the earth was not flat, as many scientists of the day believed, but actually a sphere. Even though it had not yet been proven by any man, the prophet Isaiah penned the certainty eons before: "It is He who sits above the *circle* of the earth" (Isa. 40:22). Oh, what strength and wisdom can be found by simple faith in God's Word. If He says it, I will believe it with all my might.

*Faith in the Scripture results
in fortitude of the soul.*

The foundation of skillful mapmaking was important to the aspirations of Columbus, but the next step was to put the knowledge to practical use. More than finding his way across paper with pen and ink, he had to visualize a concise path through the vast sea. He probably stared at the stars so much in preparation that he had names for them. They were the only familiar part of the journey, and you can be sure he knew them as faithful friends.

We know from his personal diaries that he sought by faith the guiding hand of the One who hung the stars in their courses. Our personal navigation has been defined as, "Looking unto Jesus, the author and finisher of our faith" (Heb. 12:2a).

It wasn't just the stars Columbus looked to; it was to the heavens.

How concerned or fearful one is about arriving at the proper destination is determined by the point of view. In Ephesians 2:6, we find the seating arrangement chosen by God for us: "and raised us up together, and made us sit together in the heavenly places in Christ Jesus." Seated *above* the circumstances of life, we look down and see that God is clearly in control.

Although his ship sailed freely and unfettered, Christopher Columbus was anchored peacefully in his heart to the steadfast rock of Christ. The man or woman who is all sail and no anchor soon finds the ship blown about by every gust of opinion and fashion. Conviction is our anchor in a tempest-tossed life.

In the days when wind was the only source of power, great importance was placed on the effective knowledge of "trimming the sail." This nautical skill enabled the sailor to make progress even if the wind departed, which is known as being "dead in the water." A good sea captain could create propulsion energy from even the gentlest of breezes as he trimmed the sails to fit the situation.

It was neither necessary nor practical to wait for a mighty wind. The same is true for the person who makes excuse after excuse about why the impossible keeps dreams hostage. The big break may never come. In that case, keep trimming the sail, using every available means at hand to continue progress. Proceed ahead, even if it is not at the swiftness you intended.

> *Slow progress is always better*
> *than no progress at all.*

PRODUCTIVITY was a by-product of years of yearning and learning. Abandoning the safety of the Old World, captain and crew pushed forward into new lands with PERSISTENCE.

PERSISTENCE

Finally, after years of planning, of begging for funds, of pleading for someone to believe with him, Columbus was ready to sail west. In 1484 he presented the plan to King John II of Portugal, who turned the plan over to a committee of experts. They did not deem the idea worthy of risk, however calculated, and rejected him. Columbus kept on seeking; he did not give up or give in. Next he turned to Spain, Portugal's great rival as a sea power. A brilliant move, I think. The young Spanish monarchs, King Ferdinand II and Queen Isabella, turned the dream over to a committee for study. Again, after a four-year waiting period, it was turned down again.

Imagine the patience and fortitude of this man. My first thought would have probably been anger. How could a committee study the dreams born in the depths of my soul or comprehend the years of calculations and intuitions from youth? Columbus kept on seeking, knocking, hoping, and praying.

At long last, in 1492, Queen Isabella agreed to finance the project. Perhaps the intrigue and mystery fascinated her to the point of agreement. I think part of it was Columbus's willingness to risk his own money, probably borrowed money at that. If you believe in yourself, you will have the ability to convince others to do so also.

Three presentations, two rejections, and years of waiting finally paid off. While some would have given up, walked away, or turned to other projects, Columbus sailed on, even if it was only in his heart.

> The heights by great men reached and kept
> were not attained by sudden flight.
> But they, while their companions slept,
> were toiling upward in the night.
>
> Henry Wadsworth Longfellow

*Persistence transforms vision
into reality.*

Nothing in the world can take the place of persistence. Talent will not; nothing is more common than unsuccessful men and women with talent. Genius will not; unrewarded genius is almost a proverb. Education will not; the world is full of educated derelicts. Persistence and determination alone are omnipotent.

Calvin Coolidge

PIETY

Adventure films and books have attempted to alter the history and heritage of the noble explorer Christopher Columbus. Undocumented charges of improper behavior cast long shadows on an otherwise shining testimony of unique character. To think what is done in private is our own business is folly. The Bible speaks of a day when the LORD ". . . will both bring to light the hidden things of darkness and reveal the counsels of the heart" (1 Cor. 4:5). Many say, "I have hurt no one. It is no consequence to anyone but me." If you can no longer trust yourself with decisions or believe in your own integrity, then it will shine through to others who will also lose faith in you. Shakespeare said, "This above all—to thine own self be true, and it must follow, as the night doth the day, thou cannot then be false to any man."

Whether the fame and fortune of Columbus's exploration turned his character, I cannot say for sure, but we know he began as a man of faith and love for the Savior.

Columbus named his first island discovery *San Salvador,* meaning "for the Savior." He said, "To the first of these islands I gave the name of the blessed Savior, San Salvador, relying upon Whose protection I reached this as well as other islands." And later he is quoted as saying, "Let it be known that these great and marvelous results are not to be attributed to any merit of mine, but to the Holy Christian Faith. . . . Therefore, let the King and Queen and all the other provinces render thanks to our Lord and Savior Jesus Christ, Who has granted to us so great a victory and such prosperity. Let Christ rejoice on earth as He rejoices in heaven in the prospect of the salvation of souls of so many nations hitherto lost."

Faith is as real as the air you breath. In fact, Hebrews 11:1 tells us, "Faith is the substance of things hoped for, the evidence of things not seen." It is not just a word you learn in Sunday school used to describe what we don't understand. It is not passed down from Mom and Dad to you. It is personal and powerful.

Columbus was taught as a boy by scholars and scientists that the world was flat. They further surmised that after so many days of sailing, the waters would become like a boiling cauldron with dangerous sea monsters living therein. No wonder he had so much trouble getting volunteers for a crew!

Columbus was presented with the paradigms of his day, and you will be persuaded to accept those of your time also. A paradigm is an accepted theory, perception, or assumption used to interpret and perceive the world.

The scholars and scientists of your days will offer you paradigms every bit as bizarre as Columbus faced. Don't be fooled by the "politically correct" movement, which infringes upon every dream with a set of absolutes predetermined by others. Those who prefer revisionism over reality, politics over fact, rhetoric over results will attempt to rewrite history to fit within their frame of ideals.

Even a casual review of our most popular classroom history books will reveal that patriotism, religion, and morality have been exorcised from our understanding. This is a systematic effort to destroy our roots by slandering our heroes.

A perfect example of this censorship in the name of blandness is the commotion over the five hundredth anniversary of Columbus's voyage to the New World. Celebrations were canceled and only sterile, unemotional commemorations were allowed in their place. This for a man who in one bold stroke expanded the unknown into the known and thereby changed the course of the world. Pioneers always take the arrows, and the pointmen always take the bullets.

Watch out for the *social* paradigm of "Everybody's doing it. If you want it, don't deny yourself. Go for it." The *scientific* paradigms assume that you agree with the theory of evolution and accept the situational ethics behind abortion, euthanasia, and legalization of drugs. As soon as the next wave of persuasion flows through, these will be recognized as being as empty and misleading as the dragons and sea monsters of old. Of course, by that time, public opinion will present another set of presumptions for you.

Don't let the circumstances or the crowd ever turn you away from what you know is right. Your goal is to discover and explore new worlds, not to argue with and alter what is already before us.

While darkness loomed in endless parade before him and many of the crew died, Columbus began to waver in his courage. The remaining crew begged him to "turn back before we all perish!" Indeed, he was surrounded by negative, complaining quitters.

But one man, his first mate, Joaquin Miller, remained faithful to the vision. He penned these words of encouragement to the lonesome pioneer:

> My men grow mutinous day by day;
> What shall I say, brave admiral, say,
> If we sight naught but seas at dawn?
> Why, you shall say at break of day:
> "Sail on! Sail on! Sail on! And on!"
>
> They sailed and sailed, as winds might blow,
> Until at last the blanched mate said:
> "Should I and all my men fall dead.
> These very winds forget their way.
> For God from these dread seas is gone.
> Now speak, brave admiral, speak and say . . ."
>
> "Sail on! Sail on! Sail on! And on!"
> Then, pale and worn, he kept his deck
> and peered through the darkness and then a speck—

A light! A light! A light!
It grew to be time's burst of dawn.
He gained a world;
he gave that world its grandest lesson:
    "On! Sail on!"

On the journey into uncharted waters, the very core of your beliefs and motivations will be challenged. It is possible and probable that in the name of scholarship the Bible will be protested. The validity of your Christian faith and all you hold to be true and dear will be doubted publicly. The "experts" will say, "It can't be so."

My own study of the word *expert* may not have its root in the Latin, but it certainly lives on in the practical: *ex* meaning "has been"; *spurt* meaning "drip under pressure." Need I say more? I am not advocating disrespect for learned men and women, but I am standing against a deterioration of the faith through intimidation and attack on the Word of God.

The life of Christopher Columbus presents a clear example of the ability to live and think in the future tense. There is no need to wait on the future—you are creating it now, today, with every word and deed.

---

*One does not discover new lands without consenting
to lose sight of the shore for a very long time.*
Andre Gide

4

PEARL HARBORED

President Franklin D. Roosevelt declared December 7, 1941, as "a date that will live in infamy." The bombing by the Japanese air force resulted in a great loss of American lives and ships at Pearl Harbor, a major U. S. naval base. War against Japan was declared within twenty-four hours in response to this devastating and unprovoked act.

Today, the U.S.S. *Arizona* stands as a memorial to the countless lives lost to the sea through this senseless act of war. There were many real-life heroes and scapegoats. Chaplain Aloysius Schmitt, of the naval ship U.S.S. *Oklahoma*, sacrificed his own life to save others. Chief Frances Day helped fifteen men to safety through a submerged porthole, losing his own life in the process. Many others acted gallantly, some whose names will never be known in this life. A total of seventy-four men received various medals of honor for their courageous deeds.

How could the Japanese have been successful in this sabotage? How could every technological device have failed to warn us? Most history books tell us it was "without warning," but there is evidence to support otherwise.

On that very day, Washington intercepted a message from Japan revealing that the attack would occur at 7:30 A.M., Hawaii time. Washington sent notification, but marked it "Routine" instead of "Urgent." Held up in State Department red tape, the cable arrived in Hawaii at 11:00 A.M. on December 7—tragically too late.

Some historians believe America was feeling invincible in her role as a superpower when the attack occurred. That's how it works in real life, too. We're on track, feeling good about the future, and then *bam!* We're suddenly hit with problems and temptations that attempt to sabotage the heart and mind.

We can learn from Pearl Harbor that our guard must always be set. Never give the enemy opportunity to trip you by offering him ammunition. Ephesians 4:27 warns: "Nor give place to the devil." Any movie, book, magazine, friend, party, or event that puts temptation into your mind is an open door to allow Satan into your life.

Secondly, never let self-assurance blind you to the possibility of an attack; never allow yourself to feel impervious to a fall. No one, save the Lord Jesus, is invincible to sin, temptation, or failure. However, we have been given the power to fight back and the ability to discern right from wrong. Don't let carelessness destroy you.

Untold thousands have looked at the fragments of a broken marriage or a wasted life only to see an urgent warning waiting nearby all along.

> Be sober, be vigilant; because your adversary the devil walks about like a roaring lion, seeking whom he may devour.
>
> 1 Peter 5:8

The term "adversary" identifies the devil as the enemy of our souls. Jesus warned Peter, "Satan has asked for you." In the book of Job, we read of Satan coming before the throne of God to ask permission to test Job.

Peter proclaims three urgent warnings against this betrayer: guard your *mind*, guard your *body*, guard your *soul*.

GUARD YOUR MIND

The command to "be sober" literally means "to build a wall of protection around and to have a mind free from intoxicants." Do not make the mistake of equating sobriety solely with alcohol abstinence. Instead of concentrating on the "can't do's," cultivate the habit of protecting yourself from temptation in everyday life. Looking at life with a clear heart and mind is essential.

Certain conditions in the environment such as fog, smog, and *vog* can hinder the clarity of a view or focus. In life, the same can be true.

Fog represents the circumstances over which you have no control. Even the most motivated and organized individuals have had their flights temporarily grounded or their trips delayed due to fog. These inconveniences are out of our control and come about through no fault of our own. As you work toward your goals, obstacles may interfere. Don't blame yourself. You had nothing to do with it! Just decide to keep going above and beyond regardless of the fog hindering your view, as the following story illustrates.

On June 15, 1815, two armed forces engaged in a life-and-death struggle at Waterloo outside of Brussels, Belgium. This was a strategic battle for the future of all of Europe. General Wellington led the charge against the infamous and much-feared General Napoleon. News of the battle was anxiously awaited by the entire country of England. All along the coast sentries were posted awaiting news of the outcome. Would England be saved or lost this day? Finally, the signal came through the mist. Anticipation gripped the heart of every man and woman as the letters were spelled out by signals from the light. The letters W E L L I N G T O N   D E F E A T were made out just before the mist became a dense fog blanketing the sky across the English Channel. Visibility of more than a few feet was impossible. Wails of discouragement and cries of despair immediately filled the land. Hours later, the fog lifted, and sentries watched for the message to come again. This time the view was clear, and the message was W E L L I N G T O N   D E F E A T E D   N A P O L E O N. This time shouts of joy could be heard for miles as neighbors ran from house to house with the news.

What a difference a clear view makes!

Smog is a by-product of pollution in the environment. In this atmosphere, protect your every breath by avoiding the polluted areas. Smog symbolizes the flagrant sin of our society. In these days of sinful rebellion, choose your company and your hangouts carefully. Make no mistake. Smog is very hazardous to your health!

Unique to the Hawaiian Islands, vog is the result of volcanic activity as the atmosphere fills with ash and pollutants. I liken it to the emotional eruptions that cloud our attitude and rob us of motivation and joy. Through anger and hurt feelings, we may lose the spirit of adventure in our everyday life. An out-of-control temper can destroy objectivity and effectiveness.

These are also the sin-habits that we seemingly can't control. They erupt when we least expect them to. By a decision of faith, we can ask God to remove our interest and affection for the destructive habit. Repentance involves a change of heart and mind about the sin. Without it, you can only rise in your own strength.

GUARD YOUR BODY

"Be vigilant" is translated "to be morally alert." This is more than saying no to sexual advances. It is carefully thinking through where to go on a date, who to go with, and what situations to be in. The New Testament Greek defines *virtue* as "moral excellence." It describes a life characterized by the control of natural appetites and a commitment to the purpose of God.

The entertainment and music industry wields an amazing amount of influential power over this generation, more than even the church or the home. The multibillion-dollar enterprise has as its agenda to blind its customers with the glitter of the "good" life. In the medium of MTV music videos, movies, and television sitcoms, sexual promiscuity is promoted as appealing, satisfying, and safe. In the hundreds of implied or portrayed sexual relations in a day of television programming, only a very small percentage of the characters will become pregnant or contract AIDS (Acquired Immune Deficiency Syndrome) or STDs (sexually transmitted diseases). In light of the millions of dollars being spent on research into venereal disease, this seems ridiculous.

Heart to heart, let me warn you: Trust God and God alone for the advancement of your social life. It makes no sense to trust Him for eternal life but not for dating and marriage. As your Creator, He knows your needs and desires. He sees your tomorrows the way you recall this morning.

An evening can start innocently and with good intentions, but end in shame and despair. "I'll just try *one* drink. It can't hurt." "We've been dating for so long, and I know we'll marry one day. Sex just this once won't hurt." "Just once" has been known since the beginning of time as a pair of dangerous words on the journey of life. The first step usually determines the next, and once you have unleashed the power of sexual and fleshly appetites, it is extremely difficult to loosen oneself from their powerful grip. The momentary mistake can lead to years of emptiness and emotional pain.

When God warned us to "Flee sexual immorality" (1 Cor. 6:18), His intention was not to cramp your fun. He saw what we didn't. According to CNN (Cable News Network), over one million people are now infected with the HIV virus leading to AIDS. AIDS is literally destroying people's lives by sucking the health from their bodies. One out of every one hundred men and one out of every eight hundred women are infected. Every 13.4 minutes someone contracts HIV. That someone could be you or a close friend—the statistics are frightening. And AIDS is really only the beginning. There are thirty-nine sexually-transmitted diseases, many of which have *no* cure. The teen pregnancy rate is skyrocketing; perhaps its fuel is the graphic sex education presented in the schools.

Don't play games with stuff that plays for keeps.

God has set a moral goal for every young person of commitment to His purpose. Don't allow yourself to be Pearl Harbored in a moment of indecision. I have derived this verb from the proper noun to graphically illustrate the potential destruction of a bad decision.

Lenny Bias, for instance, was a young man whose poor decisions destroyed him. Brought up in an outstanding family, he graduated from college and signed an incredible contract as the first-round draft choice of the NBA Boston Celtics. He was popular with fans and financially secure. He was "on top of the world." He was, however, Pearl Harbored into a night of partying with the wrong crowd and tragically robbed of the rest of his life through a reaction to crack cocaine.

Outstanding all-star Erwin "Magic" Johnson enjoyed twelve magic years of success with the Los Angeles Lakers before he was "Pearl Harbored" at the prime of his life. He had it all—the looks, the money, the adoration of fans, and love. One tragic choice affected the rest of his life, for now he struggles with AIDS.

It's true, the heart craves intimacy and a sense of belonging through companionship. But when control of the craving is given up, a moment of passion can give in to blatant disregard of the promiscuity's potentially tragic consequences. That is why Peter so urgently warns us to be morally "on guard" at all times and to keep ourselves mentally free of intoxicants. Intoxicants are not only found in alcohol and drugs but also in powerful thoughts and desires.

GUARD YOUR SOUL

One can be successful in the areas of moral purity, academic achievement, and social popularity and yet miss the most important aspect of life. "For what will it profit a man if he gains the whole world, and loses his own soul?" (Mark 8:36). There is a spiritual part of you demanding some type of fulfillment.

Notice Peter's use in 1 Peter 5:8 of the terms "adversary" and "the devil." This particular enemy is more dangerous than an army of soldiers because his attack is for all eternity. Peter emphatically stresses the urgency of "casting all your care upon Him [God], for He cares for you" (1 Peter 5:7).

If you have already been Pearl Harbored in your moral life, the experience of salvation is available to cleanse and heal you. The battle for your soul has already been fought and won at Calvary. Now you must stand up in celebration of the victory by giving Christ your heart today and forever.

5

ABOVE AND BEYOND

That which is above knows that which is below, but
that which is below will never know what is above.

Anonymous

Congratulations! As Genie said to Rugman in the hit movie
Aladdin, "Give me some tassle. Ya-yo!" By picking up this book
and beginning to read, you have declared a commitment to excellence. If altitude determines attitude, then join me in declaring,
"I am anxious to mount up with wings like an eagle to soar
above and beyond the circumstances of life." Soaring high—
such majesty. Soaring with power and grace—such motivation.
The symbol of the eagle has inspired throughout the ages.

Eagles fly higher and faster than any other bird. Nothing
average or routine about this flight pattern. It is unique in every way. Once you've seen an eagle in flight, you immediately
understand why it is called "the monarch of the sky." Its unique
wing structure allows it to reign supreme in the heavens. No
living creature, save man, can conquer it.

Its majesty and grandeur has inspired men from cave dwellers to Belshazzar of Babylon, from Caesar to Charlemagne, from Napolean to modern-day CEOs. No wonder athletes and executives alike choose to visualize themselves embodied in this regal creature. The Lord chose this favorite symbol of strength and honor to illustrate the grace and power available to us as we commit to trust His timing and the provision of His hand.

> But those who wait upon the LORD
> Shall renew their strength;
> They shall mount up with wings like eagles,
> They shall run and not be weary,
> They shall walk and not faint.
>
> Isaiah 40:31

I heard *Through the Bible* radio personality J. Vernon McGee discuss the events surrounding a fund-raising message on the Isaiah 40:31 text.

The pastor declared, "Brethren, this church needs to walk and not faint."

One of the deacons said, "Amen!"

This gave him confidence, and he continued with even more boldness, "Brethren, this church needs to run for the Lord and not be weary."

This time the deacons responded in a chorus of "Hallelujah!"

Finally, the minister thundered forth: "Brethren, this church needs to fly on wings like an eagle."

The deacons stood to their feet and cheered in unison, "Amen and hallelujah!"

"But," the preacher continued, "flying has a high price to be paid. It will cost a lot to make this church fly."

Sitting down as quickly as they had jumped to their feet a moment earlier, the deacons cooly replied, "Let her walk, brother; let her walk."

That seems to be the issue with most goals, doesn't it? What price are you willing to pay personally to soar above the routine and the ordinary? Victory is not available at discount prices.

Five basic steps will take you down the runway for liftoff:

1. Associate with successful people.
2. Avoid the pleasure seekers.
3. Anticipate periods of stress.
4. Abide in the profitable Scriptures.
5. Accentuate the positive.

ASSOCIATE WITH PEOPLE WHO ARE SUCCESSFUL

The atmosphere of your inner circle of friends is determined by your personal choices. I prefer to associate with people who are committed to integrity and motivated in goal setting. Because I want to hold myself accountable to God and to my personal goals, I have chosen to surround myself with the counsel of godly men. Twice a year we meet to review where the ministry is headed, what works and what doesn't, and to pray together. I know they are praying for me, and I pray for them daily. These men have become more than friends; they are partners with me in the ministry.

Much of my personal motivation and attitude toward success has been gleaned from the various friends and mentors who have influenced me through the years. As a young man, I had big dreams of accomplishing great things for God. My head told me my lack of knowledge and experience would hold me back. My heart told me—"We can change that!" The most obvious change was the proper education, but I also developed a plan of further education that has benefited me tremendously.

At my own expense, I traveled to meet and spend time with great men of God of various ages. Many of those early meetings turned into personal friendships, prayer partners, and mentoring relationships that I have enjoyed for years. From some I caught a fresh vision; from others I learned patience and fortitude; some showed me great insights into the walk of faith. Most of all, I developed valuable friendships that I count among my valuable assets.

Who you associate with is one of the few decisions of life over which you have 100 percent control. Pray for godly, motivated friendships, and take the time to develop them. When I take the time to enjoy relationships, I never want to worry about whether the conversation will be negative or off-color jokes will be told. When I relax, the creative juices start to flow. Being with other innovative thinkers enables me to try out new ideas and in turn offer suggestions for their plans. In the end, we've encouraged and equipped one another toward a goal and had a great time doing it! Hang with the high flyers; soar with the eagles.

Paul hung out with Barnabas for much the same reason. They brought out the best in one another. The name *Barnabas* means "son of encouragement." The two shared dreams, desires, and goals. The widow Ruth chose to live with her mother-in-law Naomi rather than return to her pagan land. On more than one occasion, Jonathan, David's closest friend, inspired him to choose God's plan. Mary Magdalene, Mary the mother of James, and Salome were together when they discovered the joyous evidence of Christ's resurrection. Joshua and Caleb stood together when all the children of Israel wanted to give up and turn back from entering the Promised Land.

Defeated people lead others to distractions, disappointment, and draining of the emotional batteries. Some will latch on to your positive spirit and be transformed. Others will just try to bring you down to their level of melancholy. These you must avoid with fervor. Please understand me. As a Christian, be kind to everyone in your path. In relationships, however, share like values and passions. Beware of those who drive in the fast lane of Excuse Expressway with no intention of using the exit ramp. A case of acute "excusitis" can be highly contagious. The "if only" handicap causes permanent damage to the motivation when appearance and circumstance become more important than accomplishment.

Two kinds of people will cross your path throughout life. They will be either *givers* or *takers.*

Givers enjoy "sharpening" your success as much as they do their own. With them I learned to surround myself with men (because I am a man) who are very committed to the Lord and high achievers in their own fields of endeavors. The most successful people I know are gracious, humble, people-helpers. They live by this truth: "Success is achieved as you enable others to become successful."

> As iron sharpens iron,
> So a man sharpens the countenance of his friend.
>
> Proverbs 27:17

Takers are usually looking for a handout, a shortcut, or a favor. I have come to the conclusion that takers are almost always rehearsing for a solo performance. Their constant song is "Me, me, me, me, me, me, me." The taker rarely listens or asks about you.

AVOID THE PLEASURE SEEKERS

Cyndi Lauper made the song "Girls Just Wanna Have Fun" popular, and it's true most teens do "just wanna have fun." Happiness is actually a very healthy attitude toward life. Jesus introduced the purpose of His ministry in John 10:10 with these words: "I have come that they may have life, and that they may have it more abundantly." His desire for you is joy and contentment in life.

If you know me at all, you know I enjoy having a laugh and a good time. The pleasure seekers, however, define fun and happiness as self-fulfillment. Their search for pleasure extends beyond fun into an addictive attitude of fulfilling desire at any cost. A pleasure-seeker goes beyond simple enjoyment into an addiction of "feel-good" activities. Beware of joining them by giving your love to unworthy things or habits.

2 Timothy 3:1–5 defines them thus:

> But know this, that in the last days perilous times will come: For men will be lovers of themselves, lovers of money, boasters, proud, blasphemers, disobedient to parents, unthankful, unholy, unloving, unforgiving, slanderers, without self-control, brutal, despisers of good, traitors, headstrong, haughty, lovers of pleasure rather than lovers of God, having a form of godliness but denying its power. And from such people turn away!

Each of these undesirable attitudes carries its own destruction and despair. When you recognize one in a person, proceed cautiously with the relationship. If you find yourself in any of the following categories, begin immediately to correct and improve.

Lover of self. Believe in yourself and love yourself, but not to the exclusion of others. Show me someone wrapped up in himself, and I'll show you an exceedingly small package. This person is self-centered and thinks the world revolves around him. This is especially true in the area of moral purity and dating. If your date does not share your commitment to moral excellence, this lover of self may try to force you to compromise for the sake of self-pleasure.

Lover of money. Notice that it is not the money that is evil; for money can be quite useful and good. Money and the sharing of it have always been in God's plan. His intention is for you to be successful and enjoy the benefits of your hard work. It was through the wealth of a businesswoman named Lydia that the first church of Phillipi was established. God blessed Abraham for his faith and faithfulness, and he became a very wealthy man. Solomon was one of the richest men to ever live. Joanna, the wife of Chuza, Herod's steward, shared the abundance of her possessions to provide for the needs of the Lord Jesus.

In Malachi 3:10, God challenged the people with a dare:

> "Bring all the tithes into the storehouse,
> That there may be food in My house,
> And prove Me now in this," says the LORD of hosts,
> "If I will not open for you the windows of heaven
> And pour out for you such blessing
> That there will not be room enough to receive it."

The excuse that "I can't afford to give my money away" is as popular today as it was in ancient times. But the Creator of all resources scoffs at such a meager justification. Refusing to share financial bounty is the quickest way to lose it.

Jesus validated financial investment in the parable of the talents. He taught of beginning with little and through hard work and wise choices multiplying it into much. To the servant who chose to invest wisely, He said: "Well done, good and faithful servant; you have been faithful over a few things, I will make you ruler over many things. Enter into the joy of your lord" (Matt. 25:23).

It is invalid to believe that we must be poor to be in God's will. Our only poverty should be in the area of selfishness and sin. A distortion of His bounty occurs when the reward becomes more dear than the Rewarder, when the blessing is sought after more than the Blesser.

It is the love of money that is the root of evil (1 Tim. 6:10). These people will sell out family, friends, and even themselves for money.

Boasters, proud. Boasters measure their self-image by accomplishment and acceptance. They brag about everything and anything, embellishing as they go to improve the story if necessary. Self-praise is on their mind at all times. Even if you wanted to compliment a taker, you couldn't get a word in!

Blasphemous. This is literally to use the Lord's name in vain, by lying, swearing, or having a filthy mouth. Since our Lord's name is to be called on for salvation, it seems ludicrous to use His holy name for cursing.

> Therefore God has highly exalted Him and given Him the name which is above every name, that at the name of Jesus every knee should bow, of those in heaven, and of those on earth, and of those under the earth.
>
> Philippians 2:9–10

The power of the name of God is wondrous. We must not disregard or defame Him simply because those around us do.

When you think about it, why do people use filthy language to punctuate remarks? Is it because their word is not effective on its own? The Bible tells us to "Let your 'Yes' be 'Yes,' and your 'No,' 'No.'"

Teenagers especially try to prove their "coolness" by using cuss words and perverted language. If the company you run with is impressed by this, you are definitely in the wrong group.

The book of James established an effective argument against foul language:

> It [the tongue] is an unruly evil, full of deadly poison. With it we bless our God and Father, and with it we curse men, who have been made in the similitude of God. Out of the same mouth proceed blessing and cursing. My brethren, these things ought not to be so.
>
> James 3:8–11

Be known for speaking truth and not trash. As the star of *Wayne's World* said to his costar Garth when he used profanity, "You kiss your mother with that mouth?"

Disobedient to parents. I meet teens across the country who risk losing the intimacy of the parent-child relationship because they don't like the rules. This is extreme selfishness. The problem is not new. Shakespeare said, "Nothing is sharper than a serpent's tooth than an ungrateful child."

Believe and understand that God has chosen the parent-child relationship as the way He can best work in our upbringing. He uses parents' love, fears, warnings, experience, and restrictions to protect us from unnecessary temptations. You are entering the time of life when more independence will be available to you, and it should be. You will soon be on your own in paying bills, making decisions, and planning the future.

In the meantime, you will be torn between some parts of life in which you must still submit to your parents. We are commanded many times in the Scriptures to obey our parents, to honor our fathers and mothers. Without this foundation, we will never be able to experience the harmony in relationships with our parents that God intended. Respect for your parents and their feelings and opinions will never change—no matter how independent or what age you become.

Maturity will respond and communicate. Immaturity will demand and pout.

Unthankful. Did you ever notice how some people can go for long periods of time without thinking of or mentioning God? Then, as soon as something goes wrong, *bam!* "Why did God do this to me?" The Bible talks over and over of the value of a grateful heart and the blessings of God that result.

The psalmist declared, "I will bless the LORD at all times;/ His praise shall continually be in my mouth" (Ps. 34:1).

Unholy. Is holiness perfection? No, it is striving to be like Jesus. To be unholy is to be unlike God in attitudes and affections.

Truce breakers. "Let your 'Yes' be 'Yes' and your 'No,' 'No.'" Always keep your word, whether it is an oath to God or a promise to a friend. A person who breaks his word in one area rattles emptiness and is not worthy to be trusted in any area.

False accusers. It is not within your responsibility to pronounce a person's actions as true or false.

Lack of self-control. We have a God-given power to control ourselves. This sets us apart from the animals. Can you say "choices"?

Brutal or fierce. In the Greek, this term describes a fierce animal that tears a victim apart. Out-of-control anger or retaliation falls into this category.

Traitor. Loyalty is one of most coveted characteristics an employer looks for in an employee. Be loyal first to the spirit of Christ, and He will direct you in each situation.

Heady. "My way or the highway" people have little tolerance for the needs of others. Stubbornness consumes them.

Boasters. Have you ever heard someone brag about things he or she should be ashamed of?

Proud. Too proud to ask for help from God or man, many people struggle in emptiness.

Haughty. "Let every man think more highly of others than of himself." Haughtiness is looking down on others. It is the exact opposite of everything the Lord Jesus taught or lived.

These traits certainly do not paint a lovely portrait, yet they are a composite of many young lives. A casual glance at any day's newspaper or evening news screams of shocking date rapes, murders, theft, drunk drivers, gangs, drug deals, etc. All these begin in the heart of the one addicted to pleasure.

Before you start to come down heavy on the above-described pleasure seeker, be aware that any of us are capable of one or more of these character traits. The Bible tells us to look into the mirror of our hearts often for "man's heart is desperately wicked." None of us is immune to undesirable traits ruling and invading our spirits. We certainly can, however, decide to make their reign short-lived!

ANTICIPATE PERIODS OF STRESS

It's been said that the only thing you can count on for sure is that things will change! Kind of a surprise guarantee! Having to prove yourself daily in the workplace, academically, and socially can cause great stress. College life may add to this life of "living on the edge." According to a 1994 *U.S. News College Guide,* almost one-quarter of all freshman at four-year colleges now report feeling overwhelmed. "The word on the street is that folks are walking into college counseling centers looking more unhappy, impaired, and dysfunctional than ten years ago," says Allan Schwartz, associate professor of psychiatry and chief of counseling and mental health services at University of Rochester in New York.

Actually, there are two types of stress: distress, which is bad, and eustress, which is good. Eustress motivates us to action as a positive force of energy impelling from within. We are motivated to do our best and to accomplish the goal. Distress is destructive physically and emotionally because it produces a negative pressure. Both types make us physically weary, but one leaves in its walk a frown, the other a tired smile of fulfillment.

Stress is also an engineering term describing the forces on materials in a building or bridge. Biologist Hans Selye says, "Stress is essentially the wear and tear of living." Some in the medical field have dubbed stress as the fastest-growing disease in the world. Still others say stress contributes to 75 percent of all illness.

David knew about stress. In Psalm 4:1, he gives praise to God: "You have relieved me in my distress." This is a picture in the Hebrew of an army trapped and surrounded in a small area by the enemy. David thanks God for enlarging his emotional and spiritual breathing space. Stress captures us and holds us hostage, but God makes room for us to breath, grow, and even enjoy life during times of distress.

Life is a bountiful rose garden of beauty—right down to the thorns and fertilizer! The days ahead will be like a luxury trans–Atlantic cruise: watch out for rough seas and storms.

Whether the stress is self-inflicted (procrastination, poor choices), produced by others, or permitted by God, He is able to preserve and deliver you. Memorize the promise of renewable strength found in Isaiah 40:31. This "natural resource" cannot be depleted for its source. Have patience in God's plan and give praise to Him from the heart. The result is tremendous power over the circumstances. The Godhead is a trinity—think of Him as your Strength, Song, and Salvation.

ABIDE IN THE PROFITABLE SCRIPTURES

The race for the twenty-first century is on, and forces are rocking the planet in anticipation! Rapid change forces technology to update constantly. If you want a great future, you must prepare for it spiritually, educationally, relationally, and vocationally.

Let's save the spiritual for last and first address education and vocation.

Author John Naisbitt predicts a successful individual in the future will need to be trilingual: fluent in Spanish, English, and computers. The Spanish language is spoken second in the world only to English. Every function of the business world is now communicated through computers. Without this skill, you will be lost in the information explosion of the twenty-first century. Because efficiency will mean the push of a button to run a program, effectiveness will become the measurement of achievement. An efficient person does things right; an effective person does the right things.

As I travel around the world, I find other countries demanding their young people to study two or three languages from childhood through high school. Advanced algebra, calculus, and geometry are considered essential to problem solving, and a twenty-five page essay of persuasion is thought to be a nominal task. A new realism is demanding more of us than ever before in the area of education.

Although I agree with Mr. Naisbitt's example of the necessary trilingual education, I go a bit further. The successful Christian must be quadrilingual, that is, fluent in Spanish, English, computer language, and the Bible. In *The Dictionary of Cultural Literacy*, author E. D. Hirsch states, "No one in the English-speaking world can be considered literate without a basic understanding of the Bible." We are not only to be fluent in its understanding and usage but also to "abide" therein. "Abide" means to turn aside from one's own way and turn to the way of another. It also indicates the intention to lodge in a particular place.

To abide in the Scriptures, an individual would turn to the Lord for instructions with the intention of basing the rest of his or her life on those principles. The Scriptures, though ancient, are profitable in enabling us to live skillfully. Even if information were to increase at the speed of light, the Bible would still be beneficial to the everyday life of man. Although technology may change, the emotions of the heart and the need for basic moral values will always remain the same.

The controversy over teaching the Bible in our schools does not diminish its power or change its central position in our culture. Far from being illegal or undesirable, teaching the Bible is both consistent with our Constitution and essential to our literacy.

The practical benefits of the Bible, though valuable, pale in comparison to its spiritual and eternal value. In it you find the words not only of life, but of eternal life. True wisdom begins with the respect of God and it transforms the spirit. Consider 2 Timothy 3:16–17:

> All Scripture is given by inspiration of God, and is profitable for doctrine, for reproof, for correction, for instruction in righteousness, that the man of God may be complete, thoroughly equipped for every good work.

Should you still have doubt, read the words of the Lord Jesus from Matthew 4:4:

> It is written, "Man shall not live by bread alone, but by every word that proceeds from the mouth of God."

ACCENTUATE THE POSITIVE

Former British Prime Minister Margaret Thatcher was asked how she maintained her positive and optimistic outlook, considering the extreme pressures of her office. This usually reserved woman gave a humorous reply: "I keep the words to a Broadway musical in my mind: 'Accentuate the positive and minimize the negative.' " Good advice for any country or position, don't you agree? It may not be set to music, but Philippians 4:8 expands the good advice into great inspiration to live by:

> Finally, brethren, whatever things are true, whatever things are noble, whatever things are just, whatever things are pure, whatever things are lovely, whatever things are of good report, if there is any virtue and if there is anything praiseworthy— meditate on these things.

The following article, dubbed "Doubt Rebuked," came across my desk recently. With startling reality it presents evidence for the achiever's cry of "Never say never!"

The following statements are taken from official documents, newspapers, and magazines widely read during their day. Listen to what the "authorities" had to say:

1840 —"Anyone traveling at the speed of thirty miles per hour would surely suffocate."

1878 —"Electric lights are unworthy of serious attention."

1901 —"No possible combination can be united into a practical machine by which men shall fly."

1926 —(from a scientist) "This foolish idea of shooting at the moon is basically impossible."

1930 —(another scientist) "To harness the energy locked up in matter is impossible."

Today —Fill in the blanks. What is the dream people tell you can't be done? Set out to achieve it!

Fortune 500 executive Steven Brown defines the situation succinctly: "In essence there are two actions in life: performance or excuses. The choice is yours." The only one who can hinder you from reaching the full potential God has uniquely designed for you is the person you see in the mirror each morning—YOU! Mount up and soar today!

6

WINDOWS OF OPPORTUNITY

*T*he *New Illustrated Space Encyclopedia* defines a *window* as "The good period or place at which activities may be conducted when otherwise requirements would be impossible or highly limiting as a minimum energy planetary launch window." You are passing by that window even now—the "good period" for reaching new successes and achievements. The nineties is the decade of enormous potential. Throughout history the last decade of a century and the first five years of the next have produced an incredible record of people endowed with astonishing creativity, inventiveness, and power.

The dawning of a new millennium has an unusual and mesmerizing effect upon mankind. This is especially true of the year 2000: "For centuries that monumental symbolic date has stood for the future and what we shall make of it. In a few short years, that future will be here," reminds John Naisbitt, author of *Megatrends 2000*. The approach of this dawning of a new millennium serves as a powerful magnet inviting us rapidly into the twenty-first century.

A few years ago, *Omni* magazine published an article entitled "End of the Century Effect" that I found particularly intriguing and memorable. My eyes were opened to the possibility of experiencing the most promising and hopeful decade in history. Skim with me through five hundred years of history, discovery, and transformation that I trust will captivate your imagination. We will gain valuable insights to the boundless potential available to us through the end-of-the-century effect.

1490s

In the final years of the fifteenth century, a flowering of creativity began to reshape the world. Da Vinci painted *The Last Supper*, and Michaelangelo began his famous *Pieta* commissioned by Lorenzo de Medici. The extraordinary styles of these famed artists have never been duplicated, and five hundred years later they remain familiar to even a schoolchild.

Copernicus studied astronomy at the University of Cracow and established a line of thought that would change man's view of himself forever. He is responsible for laying the foundation for space exploration through his teachings and writings. What then seemed absurd has now become an integral part of man's bold new world of exploration. Leonardo Da Vinci took his artistic talents one step further and created the first conceptual aircraft.

Just north of the Italian border, Martin Luther ignited the Great Reformation as he understood for the first time the realities of God's grace by faith. Climbing steps on his knees, he suddenly stood, thereby taking the first steps toward freedom of religion. A great deal of the freedom to choose a Protestant religion was conceived in that moment.

Ignatius of Loyola was nine years old when the century came to a close, but in the next one he founded the Jesuit order, bringing the name of Christ to China for the first time. And every school child knows the name of Christopher Columbus, the once-unknown sailor who fearlessly crossed an uncharted Atlantic to discover America. What uncharted waters will *you* sail into as the end of the century approaches? There is much yet to be discovered!

1590s

This was a period of great scientific discovery, conquest, and unparalleled outpouring of literary works. Galileo published his first works. After nearly a century of dormancy, the Copernican revolution was revived, and by 1600 no one ever again doubted that the sun is the center of a solar system of countless stars.

In literature, Cervantes wrote *Don Quixote*, the first modern novel, which is still required reading for many students to this day. Shakespeare penned his sonnets and three-quarters of his plays during the last decade and the first five years into the next century.

In response to a request from the Puritans, King James allowed the commencement of the English translation of the Scriptures. The King James Version of the Bible has maintained its number-one popularity slot for almost four hundred years.

The century ended with the explosion of John Calvin's *Institutes*, and religious reformation spread through John Knox into Scotland. John Bunyan's *Pilgrim's Progress* (yes, the *same* one you had to read in high school) began circulating across the English-speaking world, shaping and preparing hearts in England and America for revival and the expansion of world missions.

1690s

In 1690 John Locke wrote his two best-known works: *Essay on Human Understanding* and *Treatises on Civil Government*. These were the well springs of our modern sense of civil rights and the inspiration for the French and American revolutions. The population of America then reached 250,000, of which most were British.

1790s

Music and the arts continued to be classical in style. Hayden wrote his greatest London symphonies and *The Creation*. Beethoven became his student in 1792 and a decade later firmly established the Romantic movement in music.

In America, Washington finished his first year of the presidency as the decade opened, and Congress had convened for the first time. In the Old World, the French Revolution shaped the face of the entire century. As the decade began, Napoleon was yet an unknown student in military school; when it ended, he had carved up Italy and Egypt in bloody battles. In 1800 he established himself as the First Consul of France.

Modern missions began through William Carey and the founding of the Baptist Missionary Society in London in 1792. This quiet shoemaker with an overwhelming burden for a lost world became God's model of an innovative, indefatigable church planter. He was responsible for translating the Scriptures into five Asian languages.

1890s

In the United States of America, unimagined wealth for some followed the industrialization of the North and the use of cheap labor by immigrants; we began to be a world market power. Modern science was born. Röntgen discovered the x-ray in 1895, Rutherford found that electricity and magnetism were one, and Ramsay's multiple discoveries included the electron.

A peace-oriented German-American by the name of Einstein was now hard at work on the theory of relativity and would give birth to the deadly atomic age. Two bicycle repairmen, the Wright brothers, dreamed of manned flight, and dreams soared into reality at Kittyhawk.

Three different men were used to shape the course of Christian evangelism in the last half of the century: General William Booth, founder of the Salvation Army, and Charles Spurgeon and Dwight L. Moody, who brought the gospel to the masses. Moody's boldness through public invitation reached tens of thousands and pervaded most twentieth-century evangelism. Another visionary, missionary Dr. Hudson Taylor, was at the point of a floodtide of new missionary recruits from the United States, Canada, and Europe. Taylor's faith enabled him to mobilize a thousand missionaries through his China Inland Mission.

1990s

This narrative is yet to be written, and there is nothing stopping you from being prominently mentioned! God has always impacted history through ordinary people willing to be channels for extraordinary faith. That includes you! As a new Christian, I read this quote by Dawson Trotman and have tried ever since to live by it:

> Never do anything that someone else can or will do, when there's so much to be done that others can't or won't do.

Do not hesitate to ask big things of God; He cannot falter in His ways.

As this brief overview of history has proven, we are living today at the most opportune time ever. With the foundations of great innovation and technology already laid, we can continue to build into a limitless future. *Opportune* literally means "a favorable wind blowing the ship toward its port of destination." However, this wind can sometimes blow against you in the opposite direction. This becomes "circumstance." In Latin, the word is *circumstare*, from *circum*, meaning "around" and *stare* or "to stand." Literally, it describes our standing around while we wait for the condition or circumstance to blow us into success.

The great devotional writer J. Oswald Chambers wrote, "We are not responsible for the circumstances we are in, but we are responsible for the way we allow those circumstances to affect us; we can either allow them to get on top of us, or we can allow them to transform us into what God wants us to be. We talk about circumstances over which we have no control. None of us have control over our circumstances, but we are responsible for the way we pilot ourselves in the midst of things as they are."

Before you start each day, while your thoughts are free and clear from distraction, commit yourself afresh and anew to the will of God and to virtuous living.

A daily commitment is essential because the window of opportunity may close at any time. *Carpe diem*—"seize the day"—lest another snatch the opportunity God meant for you. Have you ever been sitting in the mall parking lot waiting patiently for a car to back out of a parking space when another driver comes charging from the other direction and whips right into *your* space? Beware of the opportunity thief. You may not see him or recognize him, but he is probably charging while you are waiting.

Indeed, every day of waiting means that a plan is in need of updating. Technology is skyrocketing; change is absolute. An average of 450 words are added to the English language each year according to *Harper's Index*. Crossing the Atlantic Ocean was once a forty-day journey. The Concorde can now accomplish the same trip 262 times during the same time period. We will be rocked repeatedly with the shocks of new technologies. The world changes swiftly, but human nature doesn't. Those who refuse to change will be as extinct as a pterodactyl caught in the tarpits of the past. Their wings continued to flap, but they never got off the ground. Keep yourself flexible and informed. It is not survival I speak of, but the same conquering spirit Columbus had when he transformed ideas and possibilities into reality with courage.

As you prepare to open the window of opportunity before you, consider the traits of the pioneers of yesterday. Obviously, a solid education is only the foundation. Even more powerful than genius is the power of a steadfast dream, the energy of a focused vision, and the tenacity to see it through to the end no matter how loud the voices of discouragement.

Christa McAuliffe, the first teacher to attempt a space mission, touched the world with her commitment to excellence. She adopted as her motto, "I touch the future; I teach." Education on a basic level will enable you to earn a living, but to this highly motivated lady teaching was far more than a paycheck. She delighted in giving the gift of self-knowledge and wisdom. McAuliffe offered her life as a teacher to her students; in bravery, she offered her life to the exploration of new frontiers. The day the *Challenger* exploded, McAuliffe's body burned with it, but her memory and gift of motivation toward discovery will continue to live on.

Discovery is the ability to look at the same situation as everyone else and yet think something different. Consider any modern invention—the discovery was a response to an idea, not the idea itself. Thomas Edison used to say, "I saw a need for something and then decided to invent it." The first person who looked at sawmill waste and saw it as a compressed fire log discovered a useful product from a seemingly useless one.

One of the most fascinating stories I have ever read in this vein is Earl Tupper's, the founder of Tupperware. Earl didn't know you couldn't overcome obstacles, so he just did. Because his family was poor, he was mostly self-educated. Perhaps this extra amount of digging into information gave him the edge to look at things in a new way. He had the inventor's spirit of discovery even as a young man.

After working in a DuPont chemical factory for many years, Tupper determined to start his own business. Having almost no capital with which to begin the venture, he began to experiment with the polyethylene slag left behind as waste after the oil-refining process was completed. No one else even remotely considered the putrid, hard substance. But Tupper never gave up. Hundreds of experiments later, he learned to purify the nasty substance and transform it into the first plastic food-storage containers. The rest, as they say, is history for the billion-dollar Tupperware industry.

Remember the unknown Napoleon who conquered the world shortly after military school? He was not the most powerful general in the world by accident. He believed that in every battle a crisis period of approximately thirty minutes would occur. During this brief opening, he theorized, the battle would be won or lost. The window of opportunity, however momentary, must be seized before it is closed.

The most vivid depiction of opportunity I have ever heard of was that of the Greeks' statue of *Janis*. On one of my trips to Athens, a guide told the story: as one approaches the statue, the lean, muscular lines and long, flowing hair are glorious in detail. When observed from behind, however, the body appears flabby and the head bald. What a graphic portrayal of opportunity as it comes to us and then as it flees undetained. Visualize the long, flowing hair reaching out its invitation and grasp it with a fierce grip of boldness. Delay doing so, and you will be left staring at it from behind with only a thought of what might have been.

Of all the words of paper and pen, some of the most tragic I recall are "what *might* have been." Never let the opportunity planned for you by God as your Creator pass you by. In the words of the Steve Miller Band, "Don't stop thinking about tomorrow. Don't stop, it will soon be here."

7

ATTEMPT SOMETHING GREAT

During the cloudy days of the Civil War, it was difficult to find joy or strength of spirit. President Lincoln would often slip into a Wednesday evening service at the New York Avenue Presbyterian Church in search of encouragement and comfort through the sermon. After one particularly dramatic presentation, his young aide asked the president his opinion. He responded concerning Dr. Gurley's message: "It was well thought out, powerfully delivered, and very eloquent." The aide said, "Then you thought it was a great sermon." "No," replied Lincoln. "It failed because Dr. Gurley did not ask us to do something great."

When former first lady Barbara Bush was asked to make the commencement speech at Wellesley College, she urged the all-women graduating class to "First, believe in something larger than yourself to get involved in some of the big ideas of the time. Second, have some fun. And, third, invest time and energy into your family."

One never knows what awaits us on the other side of the mountain, but it must be climbed anyway. Perhaps it is some very good or valuable thing. We cannot sit in the valley hoping it will move of its own accord. We might pitch a tent for a night of camping in the Valley of Decision, but we surely should not build a house there.

> *The chief tragedy in most lives is not dying, but making small what clearly could be made large. People all too frequently fill their minds with trifling matters, neglect opportunities, pursue insignificant purposes, and please themselves with things of little importance or merit. In man's small and uncaring ways, many people spend their time doing things of minimal consequence. Many people do not live big lives—they live little ones.*
>
> Elton Trueblood

Mountain climbing is not without its dangers, but it will always cause you to work a little harder and pull a little longer before giving up. I read the most inspirational story of a young man named Mark Wellman in an issue of *Time* magazine. A fifty-foot fall during a 1982 rock-climbing expedition cost him the use of his legs, but he does not think of himself as disabled. "My whole thing," says the park ranger, "whether it's kayaking, skiing or rock climbing, is finding another way." Since that fall, the "other way" took Wellman 3,569 feet up the sheer granite face of El Capitan in California's Yosemite Valley.

After months of swimming and weight training, he left his wheelchair behind and, with an occasional lift from fellow climber Michael Corbett, pulled and hauled himself to the top. He likened the feat to doing *seven thousand* pull-ups! Despite blistering heat and winds that sometimes blew the pair ten feet out from the rock, they completed their ascent in seven days—a double conquest of El Capitan and of the presumed limitations of the human body.

You also will face mountains as difficult as El Capitan: mountains of temptation, mountains of difficulty, mountains that challenge your spirit and your convictions. The preparation and strength Wellman put in made the difference between conquering the mountain or being conquered by his circumstances.

We cannot expect to climb hurdles, to beat the odds, or to stand our ground against temptation without spiritual preparation. The potency of the Word of God in your life will be determined by how much you actually read and apply it. This is the real strength training: spending time in the Word of God—"For the word of God is living and powerful" (Heb. 4:12). Spend time in prayer that you might be able to say, "I know whom I have believed" (2 Tim. 1:12).

You will then be sure of your ability because you will believe in His unfailing ability. You will not only attempt something great, you will accomplish it!

Using the *New Wilderness Handbook,* we can make an interesting comparison between the elements and techniques involved in scaling a mountain and the instruction of the Bible concerning spiritual and emotional mountain climbing. I should add that my daughter Christa is an avid indoor rock climber. She loves it! I ran these ideas by her, and she gave me two thumbs-up!

Judgment, balance of the feet, weight distribution, knowledge of the terrain, proper equipment, good physical/spiritual condition, and confidence are essential to the skill of climbing.

JUDGMENT

Before you can begin a climb, clear judgment must be executed by taking all factors contributing to safety into consideration. Is the weather severe or tolerable? Am I in good health and physically strong enough? Has proper training, warm up, and preparation been completed successfully? Do I have the proper equipment and is it in good condition?

For the spiritual climb, many of the same questions will be applied. Instead of weather, I should be concerned with my environment: friends, acquaintances, places I spend my time and money, the mental and spiritual influence I have allowed myself to be placed under. Am I spiritually healthy and right with God so that unconfessed sin cannot rob me of my joy and strength? Am I prepared through knowledge of the Word and time in prayer to use them readily as tools of accomplishment or overcoming?

BALANCE OF THE FEET

Paul Petzoldt, director of the Wilderness Education Association, says, "Aside from judgment, balance is the basis of all climbing." Balance is achieved by putting the emphasis on the footing rather than the hands. A climber concentrates on each step of his footing to be sure it is stable before using the hands to pull toward the cliff. The security of the foothold is dependent on the angle of the feet.

Balance in spiritual and moral things can seem impossible at times, especially when the tide of popularity flows against all that you stand for. God offers balance to your stance: "He makes my feel like the feet of deer, / And sets me on my high places" (Ps. 18:33). "He also brought me up out of a horrible pit, / Out of the miry clay, / And set my feet upon a rock, / And established my steps" (Ps. 40:2). Wow—God desires for us to be climbers, enables us to be climbers, and climbs along with us!

Through the wisdom of the Word and godly counsel, you have available to you balance in decisions, in daily plans, and in goals for the future. You need not walk the flat, uninteresting terrains of life. You can begin climbing at any time.

WEIGHT DISTRIBUTION

A climber can be in a safe climbing position by transferring weight from one limb to another in a smooth, flowing action. This allows the climber to release one hold at a time while maintaining the other three points of contact as the mountain is ascended. Petzoldt says a skilled climber will appear to flow up the mountain rather than move with jerks and lunges.

When Jesus said, "I will never leave you nor forsake you," he meant *never*. Not in dangerous times of climbing, not when you're getting ready to climb, not when you're coming down from a climb, and certainly not if you fall during a climb. Christa tells me the more difficult the climb, the more fun she has in the challenge and the bigger the high when she reaches the top. The way up is difficult, but that's what makes it so exciting.

You are never alone. Learning to lean on Jesus is more than a song; it's a way of life. He is strong and without fail. Learn to lean completely on Him as you give life your best shot. When He promises "My grace is sufficient for you" (2 Cor. 12:9), He is letting you know that He is all you will ever need for emotional and spiritual strength. Rely heavily on Him for each movement in the climb.

KNOW YOUR TERRAIN

Learn as much as you can about the mountain you are about to climb. When can you expect to be midway? What elevation level will you climb to? How long should it take you to reach the top or your goal point?

Spiritual battles will discourage you from continuing the climb. These obstacles to the spirit can be overcome if we understand their source: "For we do not wrestle against flesh and blood, but against principalities, against powers, against the rulers of the darkness of this age, against spiritual hosts of wickedness in the heavenly places" (Eph. 6:12).

Recognize the attack and fight accordingly. Determination is the beginning. Trusting in God is the endurance component. Patience will see you through in your attempt of the great.

EQUIPMENT

The climbing rope is the most important piece of equipment. Careful selection of the rope is vital. The climbing rope must be inspected before each and every attempt and especially after any fall. Look to see if any strands have been partially cut by falling rock, worn thin by stretched edges, or slightly weakened by prolonged exposure to the sun. No rope should be used for climbing if it has a bad nick in one or more strands. Most accidents are due to undetected rope damage.

The lifeline we have been given is never in need of damage inspection, but should be examined over and over. Jesus Himself is our lifeline, and a careful examination of His strength will cause us to gain confidence in the climb. An inventory of all that is available to you—His power, wisdom, might, love, mercy, patience, righteousness, and more—will cause you to say "I'm ready to climb. Show me that mountain!"

Here are the directions for using the climbing gear:

> Finally, my brethren, be strong in the Lord and in the power of His might. Put on the whole armor of God, that you may be able to stand against the wiles of the devil. . . . Stand therefore, having girded your waist with truth, having put on the breastplate of righteousness, and having shod your feet with the preparation of the gospel of peace; above all, taking the shield of faith with which you will be able to quench all the fiery darts of the wicked one. And take the helmet of salvation, and the sword of the Spirit, which is the word of God; praying always with all prayer and supplication in the Spirit, being watchful to this end with all perseverance.
>
> Ephesians 6:10, 14–18

Notice two things about the armor: the sexual parts of the body are covered, the back is not.

You will never climb higher than when you stand for moral purity. While the crowd of sexual permissiveness gathers at the base of the mountain, you can take one step and then another to set yourself apart from the "base" lack of self-control. Sexual purity will always be the road you must choose, whether or not you are married. God's intention from the beginning for the gift of sex was for one man to share with one woman and no one else in each lifetime. Don't judge your moral values by those of anyone else, no matter how spiritual their talk or high their station in life. The Book of Books is your unchangeable standard.

Why do you suppose your back is not covered by this armor? Remember this is not a jogging outfit with which to flee from Satan, although we are told to do so. This is the dress of a warrior, and a warrior *never* turns his back when fighting the enemy. Do not run from the battle if it needs to be fought. For example, once and for all, run through that bad habit with the Sword of the Word and never deal with it again. "Resist the devil and he will flee from you" (James 4:7). He has no armor and his power is no match.

GOOD PHYSICAL/SPIRITUAL CONDITION

Of course, a climber never begins or even thinks of beginning without good health and strong, muscular form. You cannot fight a spiritual battle or climb the mountain of success without excellent spiritual health.

Peace with God is your most important asset. When you are rightly related to Him, your sin of the past is forgiven; you have power in the present, and He is guiding and planning for your future.

Getting right with God is so very simple. Humble your heart to Him for His forgiveness is vast. "If we confess our sins, He is faithful and just to forgive us of our sins" (1 John 1:9). To "confess" means to agree with. Just to say, "Yeah, I did it" is of no consequence. God already knows you did it! Confession and repentance are synonymous. They require a change of heart and attitude toward sin-habits. If we agree with God about our sin, then we feel the same way about it as He does— that is, He *hates* it!

One reason we struggle so greatly with bad habits is because we derive a certain amount of pleasure from them. They seem impossible to put behind us because they are of great importance to our emotions or comfort. Let me illustrate it thus: If you were told, "no sweets, burgers, fries, or cokes for six months—only raw vegetables," this might be an unpleasant time for you and for those who have to live with you! On the other hand, if you were told, "no vegetables, cooked or raw, for six months, but you can have all the chocolate, sweets, fries, and burgers you can eat," you would probably not have trouble living with the plan.

What's the difference? One is tolerated, perhaps enjoyed. The other is craved and loved! (I don't think I need to explain which one.) When we ask God to change our heart about the sin-habits we crave, it will not be a difficult task to put them behind us. My wife prays, "Lord, turn this habit from chocolate to broccoli so that I will hate it!" She says it works, and it sounds like pretty good theology to me.

God hates sin, not just yours or mine, but any sin. When we reach the place where we hate it as He does, we will abandon it without regard. It is the sin we love that we are unable to overcome. Pray to this end.

CONFIDENCE

Did you know that many accidents are caused because the climber allowed fear to grip the heart and he or she looked downward long enough to fall there? When panic strikes, the climber may be tempted to cling to the mountain with hands instead of standing sure on balanced feet. This is a dangerous and exhausting situation, because the forces of gravity work against him. The climber must check the rope and be confident of its ability to control a major fall.

Three hundred and sixty-five times the phrase "fear not" appears in the Bible, one for every single day of the year. You need never falter in the midst of the climb to excellence, for you can depend on His strength, wisdom, and guidance and not solely on your self. The Christian knows the Savior is ready to come alongside in the event of a fall to catch you in His hands. David relinquished his life to God's will when he said, "My times are in your hands." God will bear you up in a fall so that you can recover quickly and climb once again.

There is one mountain that must be climbed before any others are attempted: It is the Mountain of Transformation.

> Now after six days Jesus took Peter, James, and John his brother, led them up on a high mountain by themselves; and He was transfigured before them. His face shone like the sun, and His clothes became as white as the light. And behold, Moses and Elijah appeared to them, talking with Him. Then Peter answered and said to Jesus, "Lord, it is good for us to be here; if You wish, let us make here three tabernacles: one for You, one for Moses, and one for Elijah. While he was still speaking, behold, a bright cloud overshadowed them; and suddenly a voice came out of the cloud, saying, "This is My beloved Son, in whom I am well pleased. Hear Him!"
>
> Matthew 17:1–5

The outward appearance of the Lord Jesus changed inside out right before their very eyes. Can you even imagine? The word translated "transfigured" gives us the English word *metamorphosis*. This metamorphosis occurs from the inside out and is a total, complete change of substance. When a caterpillar becomes a butterfly, it does not change clothing. It is thoroughly and completely transformed by metamorphosis.

One day it crawls in the dust and on another it floats on the winds. What a sight to behold!

This is God's intention for every person: to be so totally transformed by His power that we are able to soar above and beyond the dirt of the past and the dust of mediocrity filtering through the present. "Therefore, if anyone is in Christ, he is a new creation; old things have passed away; behold, all things have become new" (2 Cor. 5:17). He will do the same for anyone who asks by calling on His name.

God can do a new thing in you. How do I know? Because He has transformed me from barely getting by to a lover of the high places of life. There is something peaceful and wondrous about standing tall and alone in the mountains. It gives you a new perspective on problems and conquering them.

Now, "just between us girls," what is your spiritual relationship to Christ? Do you "know that you know that you know" that if you died tonight you would go to heaven? Could you stand before Him this day unashamed and ready to meet Him?

The Bible defines three basic categories of people that each of us falls under at one time or another in our lives. They are: *the natural, the spiritual, and the carnal.*

THE NATURAL

The most obvious definition of the natural man is found in 1 Corinthians 2:14: "But the natural man does not receive the things of the Spirit of God, for they are foolishness to him; nor can he know them, because they are spiritually discerned." The Greek word for "natural" here is taken from the word *soul* and refers to those who are unsaved. Everyone is born with his back toward God. For this reason Jesus taught, "Most assuredly, I say to you, unless one is born again, he cannot see the kingdom of God" (John 3:3).

Without the experience of personal, life-changing salvation, we will be destined to live only by the flesh. The "natural" person can be outwardly good-looking, letter in sports, or be on the honor roll, but that is not enough. The moral individual, the church member, the "good kid"—all need the salvation offered in Christ's death on the cross. You see, it's not what *we* can do, but what God has already done for us. Man's physical birth is not complete without the spiritual birth.

As the Scripture teaches, the spiritual cannot be *received*—this word means to welcome, to embrace, or to make possess—except by the spiritual person. Not being that spiritual person may be the root cause of the lack of faithfulness among young people in worship, Bible study, and church attendance once they are out on their own. It is only when we embrace the things of God with our hearts that they become exciting and alive to us. A "natural [teen] does not receive the things of the Spirit of God, for they are foolishness to him" (1 Cor. 2:14a). Just as the many channels on your radio can only be tuned in with the right equipment, the things of God cannot be received without salvation.

The apostle Paul divides the personality into three separate compartments:

> Now may the God of peace Himself sanctify you completely; and may your whole spirit, soul, and body be preserved blameless at the coming of our Lord Jesus Christ.
>
> 1 Thessalonians 5:23

God is a trinity, and He has created man in His image as a trinity also. We are soul, body, and spirit. The physical body receives signals from the physical environment. The soul has to do with ego, conscience, and self-awareness, and the spirit is able to receive the things of God.

THE SPIRITUAL

The apostle continues in 1 Corinthians 2:15–16 to describe the spiritual person. I remember the night as a senior in high school when I realized my condition apart from God and heard the good news that Jesus Christ had me on His mind when He died and when He rose again. I asked God to forgive and cleanse me from sin as I invited Him to come into my heart. God's spirit entered my life immediately upon being invited to do so. I offered Him control of my life.

Dr. Jerry Vines is one of the greatest pastors in our country. The growth of his church speaks in confirmation of his excellent teaching and preaching. He teaches that the Holy Spirit *resides in* the life of a spiritual person, and that the Holy Spirit *presides over* the life of a spiritual person. For this reason, the spiritual one can have assurance, insight, and genuine peace while others are uncertain, confused, and coming apart at the seams.

THE CARNAL

The third category for people is graphically described in chapter 3 of 1 Corinthians. Paul defines and describes this person as a genuine Christian who allowed selfish or fleshly desires to dominate life. These individuals are too self-sufficient or too busy for the things of God. Their lives are characterized by immaturity, envy, and strife. Paul even dubbed them "babies" because of their behavior. He later wrote in chapter 13 of Corinthians: "When I was a child I spoke, understood, and thought as someone immature. But when I grew up I put away childish things" (v. 11 paraphrase). The carnal person lives beneath the abundance promised and freely available from the hand of God. He allows the bondage of habits and poor choices to keep him grounded in life. Don't settle for scratching out an existence with the chickens in the backyard when God's desire for you is to "mount up with wings like eagles."

You can and must attempt something great for the Lord, for He has already done great things for us. Read these exciting quotes:

- Mary, the mother of Jesus sang, "For He who is mighty has done great things for me, /And holy is His name" (Luke 1:49).

- "Often the doors of opportunity swing on the hinges of obedience" (Dr. Ike Reighard, outstanding pastor and youth speaker).

- Author J. Sidlow Baxter wrote, "What is the difference between an obstacle and an opportunity? Our attitude toward it! Every opportunity has a difficulty and every difficulty has an opportunity."

- William Shakespeare wrote, "The future is an undiscovered country."

Shakespeare was only *half* right. The future is undiscovered to us, but very well known to the God who writes the future. By faith we can begin the climb to a great future pulsating with tremendous opportunities.

Begin with climbing; finish with soaring on the wings of an eagle!

8

SAY YES TO GOD'S BEST

Inner thoughts of joy and excitement crowd the mind as they wait to be audibly expressed on the final day of graduation ceremonies. Both shouts and grad caps fill the air. It is an eve of celebration. But before the next day dawns, new voices replace the thrill of graduation with confusion over the near future. "This way!" "No, no. Follow me!" "You can't go in there!" The competition between fear and adventure can be maddening as the dreams of the heart war with the doubts of the mind. Reality sets in as you attempt to move forward in new responsibilities and challenges.

"Somewhere, somehow," you think, "there must be a set of ground rules for making decisions." Yes, there are some basic directions for every Christian to begin with. The first and foremost foundation of every decision is also the sole limitation of our goal setting: it is the will of God for each life.

> GOD'S WILL—EXACTLY WHAT I WOULD
> CHOOSE IF I KNEW ALL THE FACTS.
>
> Bill Gothard

The will is defined in the Greek language as determination, choice, purpose, desire, pleasure. In fact, the will of God is that which enables us to be complete in our purpose.

> *That you may stand perfect and complete*
> *in all the will of God.*
>
> Colossians 4:12b
>
> *Make you complete in every good work to do His*
> *will, working in you what is well pleasing in*
> *His sight, through Jesus Christ, to whom be*
> *glory forever and ever. Amen.*
>
> Hebrew 13:21

Many theologians teach the will of God in three distinct parts: His moral will, His sovereign will, and His specific will for the individual. The moral will is, of course, self-evident through the many proclamations of the Scripture. "For this is the will of God, your sanctification: that you should abstain from sexual immorality" (1 Thess. 4:3). "Let every soul be subject to the governing authorities" (Rom. 13:1).

God's sovereign will is also clearly narrated throughout the pages of the Bible. The book of Revelation gives us the final judgments and eternal specifications of God's plan through the ages. This, too, is unalterable.

However, life's choices of turns and options of speeds increase as each one of us explores the great quest for life's best. The specific will of God is different for every person. Where you should go to school, who or if you will marry, what career option should be pursued—all of these have been fully thought out and planned by the Lord for you. "I believe this," you say, "but I have no clue as to what He wants for *me* at *this* time in my life."

The first requirement for finding God's will for your life is to know Him personally as your Savior. Having this assurance, you can then proceed to the next step: knowing God's will as plainly revealed to you in the Word of God.

So many times we struggle with decisions already clearly decided and stated by God. The first place to turn in seeking God's will is to the Bible itself. However, there are many aspects of life for which there are no specific biblical instructions, such as career choices, education, and timing of decisions. These must be determined by a combination of events. Above all, remember that God has infallibly promised to order "for good" the lives of those who truly love Him (Prov. 3:5–6; Rom. 8:28).

We must first obey what God has already revealed to us concerning His will for our lives. We cannot expect Him to tell us more than we have already obeyed. It is equally important to trust God for your decision, regardless of what the outcome may be. Jesus prayed, "Father, . . . not My will, but Yours, be done" (Luke 22:42). This can only be accomplished when we realize how very much God loves us and wants the best for our lives. Faith and obedience go together.

Often we seek advice on a decision only because we hope by asking many times we will eventually receive the answer *we* desire. Seeking advice is an excellent help in determining God's will, but be careful to seek *godly* counsel. Talk to your pastor, youth worker, Sunday school teacher, or other leaders in your church. God has given us parents for this very reason, so that He may speak to us through their authority and experience.

Many of us too casually inquire about God's will for our lives. If we really want God's best for us, it will become a matter of urgent prayer each day until the answer is clear. Ask yourself, "Just how much time do I spend in prayer asking God to reveal His will?" Instead, it is easier to depend on circumstances as our answer. Yes, God does use circumstances to reveal His will, but circumstances alone are not enough. Remember, God's circumstance will never be contrary to the Scriptures. The Word of God is the final word on decisions of life. However, in areas where there is no specific revelation, you must depend on prayer, circumstances, and godly counsel. One is not enough.

These must be combined with earnest trust in God for His best in life. In His time and in His way His will becomes plain.

One thing you can be sure of—it's a great plan. The plan involves your own will, emotions, and thoughts. The Creator has chosen it for you, His own creation. Here are some potential points to ponder on as you pray for understanding.

- *Start with a review of where you are in your spiritual walk.* "And do not be conformed to this world, but be transformed by the renewing of your mind, that you may prove what is that good and acceptable and perfect will of God" (Rom. 12:2).

- *Enjoy doing the will of God from the heart*—"not with eyeservice, as men-pleasers, but as bondservants of Christ, doing the will of God from the heart" (Eph. 6:6).

- *Make the pursuit of God's will a daily habit and lifestyle of being open to the will of God.* Jesus said, "Not My will, but Yours . . . " (Luke 22:42).

- *Pray for His will to be done.* "Your will be done / On earth as it is in heaven" (Matt. 6:10).

- *Be filled with the knowledge of His moral and sovereign will:* "For this reason we also, since the day we heard it, do not cease to pray for you, and to ask that you may be filled with the knowledge of His will in all wisdom and spiritual understanding" (Col. 1:9).

- *Be absolutely committed to live by the Word of God and the will of God. Accept nothing less as your standard!* "That he no longer should live the rest of his time in the flesh for the lusts of men, but for the will of God" (1 Pet. 4:2).

- *Declare the will of God as your first consideration of every goal or decision.* "Come now you who say,

'Today or tomorrow we will go to such and such a city, spend a year there, buy and sell, and make a profit'; whereas you do not know what will happen tomorrow. For what is your life? It is even a vapor that appears for a little time and then vanishes away. Instead you ought to say, 'If the Lord wills, we shall live and do this or that.'" (James 4:13–15).

- *Cultivate the attitude of gratitude in your heart.* "Rejoice always, pray without ceasing, in everything give thanks; for this is the will of God in Christ Jesus for you" (1 Thess. 5:16–18).

Looking into the mirror of God's Word is the only accurate way to take inventory of one's spiritual condition. Leaving home does not equate with leaving God. Many young people find themselves sledding downhill on the blessings God has given their parents, only to find a sudden crash as they bottom out to independence.

Remember—the way of God *cannot* be contrary to His divine Word. If the decision or goal will at any time violate the true principles of God, consider it no longer. The answer is a sure NO! When praying for wisdom, take heed to first obey what God has already revealed to you. Just as headlights give you only enough light to safely drive a short distance, so the Lord gives you just enough light to obey and sufficient faith to continue until more light appears. Although the answers depend 100 percent on God, they also rely 100 percent on your obedience and faith.

IF WE OBEY THE KNOWN, GOD WILL LEAD US IN THE UNKNOWN.

The question may linger in your minds: "Does God actually care enough to listen to me?" Knowing our concern before we ourselves were even aware of it, He sent us these words:

*But if anyone is a worshiper of God and does
His will He hears him.*

John 9:31b

*Then you will call upon Me and go and pray
to Me, and I will listen to you.*

Jeremiah 29:12

After all, there is not enough spiritual warfare in the world,
nor enough ungodly influence over men, to stop the sovereign,
supernatural will of God.

DECISION MAKING "BY THE BOOK"

Pray for the understanding of the first principles of His
will and then for the understanding to apply those principles
to your decision making—according to the will of God. Correct decisions will always glorify God. Here is a checklist for
decision making:

- Is it in accord with the moral will of God? (1 Thess.
  4:3)
- Is it in harmony with the commands, truths, and
  principles of the Word of God? (Rom. 12:2)
- Have I sought godly advice?
- Does this decision fulfill the Golden Rule?
- How will it affect my immediate relationships?
- Will the ultimate outcome bring glory to God?
- Will the result be in keeping with my priorities of
  giving my best energy?
- What is my real motive in this? Is it doing the will
  of God from the heart?

- Am I totally committed to whatever, whenever, wherever God leads me in this as I seek Him?

- Do I have total peace in my decision?

The power of a refreshed spirit and positive thoughts can energize you in the long haul. While the world defines success from the outside in, we Christians must find our significance from the inside out. Wait patiently on God! Anticipate His best for you! Choose to say, "Yes, Lord, yes to Your will and to Your way."

9

CHICKEN LITTLE WAS WRONG AGAIN!

Do you recall the story of Chicken Little? She ran around the barnyard proclaiming imminent destruction. "The sky is falling! The sky is falling!" she cried. For a short time, all of the other barnyard animals believed her prophecy of doom until they realized one chicken's fear did not make a crisis situation.

This same contagious pronouncement of despair permeates our culture today. We often hear of a "Chicken Little" crisis of confidence, particularly if the media need to drum up some interest for the sake of competition. Instead of the sky that is falling, it may be the employment rate, the stock market, or other economic factors. Perhaps it is the various skirmishes across the globe or the hatred between races that invades our home through television satellites.

From economics to environment, education, or excellence, the stability vanishes before our eyes, leaving folks puzzled about the security of the future. Senior citizens mutter, "Things aren't the way they used to be."

The headlines scream to us, "These are the worst of times": tension in the Middle East, the breakdown of peace treaties, scandal in Washington, the AIDS epidemic and health concerns, unemployment rising and falling at whim, terrorism everywhere. After a decade of the war on drugs, present-day government-appointed persons now advocate the legalization of drugs.

Traveling across the country, I collect newspapers from almost every airport stop. For the most part, I could clip off the headline identification and interchange the pages because the bad news is repeated from city to city. A nine-year-old was recently kidnapped from the safety of her own bedroom while her mother slept in the other room. An angry husband held his children hostage after murdering his wife. A disgruntled employee set off a bomb in the office building. Young soldiers said good-bye to family and friends as they were sent off from one war to another. I could continue, but I'd rather not.

Seems fairly depressing, doesn't it? It doesn't have to be. You can choose to look past the harshness of reality to the rainbow of promise awaiting you. Every generation has had its challenges. For some it was world war. For others the holocaust of disease ran rampant or the strain of poverty held them captive.

Isaac lived through two periods of famine throughout the land. He replanted the land and successfully cared for his family. Jesus had no place to lay His head, but was cared for by many friends. Mary and Joseph were forced to flee from danger into a strange land. They escaped to safety. Paul was shipwrecked, imprisoned, and scorned. He made a greater impact on biblical history than anyone who has ever lived other than Christ. Deborah led 10,000 untrained, unequipped men on a treacherous, week-long journey up to the top of a mountain. There they faced 100,000 fully trained and furnished soldiers. God gave them the victory, of course, and the enemy perished. There are countless stories of victory over the circumstances throughout the Scripture.

A survey of history, even recent, displays the strength of young men and women as they rise to walk in victory over the odds. The magical, mysterious elixir of perspiration and inspiration will always come shining through the gloom!

With those positive truths overshadowing the negative details, let us examine the challenges ahead in ECONOMICS, the ENVIRONMENT, and EXCELLENCE.

ECONOMICS

Paul Laxalt, former senator from Nevada, once told an audience of McDonald's franchisees, "Today we have a Chicken Little theory of economics. This time it isn't the sky that is falling; rather America's middle class is disappearing, vanishing before our very eyes." He refers to the prophecies by modern-day Jeremiahs who believe two economic classes will be all that remain in the imminent future—the very rich and the very poor.

These are confusing days in which to try understanding the business section of your newspaper. While one page details the great success of a company, the very next column may offer to sell a foreclosed building or failed business. This week when I asked one stockbroker when would be the best time to buy, he replied *"Last* year."

It's no wonder we are bewildered about the economy when even the experts can't agree. Here's a poignant quote by George Bernard Shaw: "If all economists were laid end to end, they would not reach a conclusion." Not to be outdone, Arthur Motley added this thought: "If all economists were laid end to end, they would point in different directions."

Debate continues to rage over a solution to the national debt, now in the trillions of dollars. All talk and very little action has produced dangerous and potentially deadly economic situations for both the country and individuals. From generation to generation, we hang it over our children's heads like a giant atomic mushroom cloud.

In actuality, though, the world *is* entering the twenty-first century in a period of economic prosperity. With free-trade agreements, the spread of democracy into former Communist and dictator governments, and the encouragement to free enterprise, more and more job opportunities will await the graduate.

> *For every door of occupation that technology closes, it will open two windows of opportunity.*

Another growth factor in the financial picture is the conversion to a global economy. This requires of us a broader vision, a more cooperative spirit, and an intense desire to better understand diverse cultures and customs. Common understanding and global perspective are no longer options; they are now imperatives for every one of us.

Begin with classroom education, but intend daily to glean an education from every situation and person in your path. If something is built on a negative premise, then you have a double bonus, because you have already learned at least one way *not to* go.

EDUCATION

With all America has going for her in reputation and resources, why would we be labeled "a nation at risk"? The National Commission on Excellence in Education, a key blue-ribbon panel, gave this report: "The educational foundations of our society are presently being eroded by a rising tide of mediocrity. We have, in effect, been committing an act of unthinking, unilateral education disarmament." This is an extreme national tragedy.

Not only is the quality of education a major concern, but the safety of our schools has eroded into a battle zone. Many public schools now employ at least one police officer to patrol the halls. Locker inspections and confiscations of guns are everyday practices.

Both scholarship and security are becoming so inferior that one individual offered to donate $500 million in an effort to improve education and stem the violence.

One net result is the many graduates who are not prepared for the work force. Today companies are setting up classrooms to train employees in the most basic of educational skills with high school remedial classes. Colleges have had to re-engineer many degree programs to include remedial studies. This has been cited as one of the primary reasons why 46 percent of college students extend their attendance from four years to six or more for the same degree.

Rarely do students debate the necessity of college these days. Now the question is "How much further do I go?" The new generation of business persons is an ultra-educated force of masters-degree-carrying achievers. Almost equal in popularity is the alternative education found in specialized business and vocational schools, particularly in the field of computer technology. Many large companies have their own schools and will train new employees on their specific equipment and programs.

Almost all companies, regardless of their size, are providing motivational and relationship seminars either in-house or by joining with other groups and businesses.

Having established the framework of your further education, move on in your concentration beyond facts and figures to thinking and retention techniques. Learn *how* to learn and keep on learning. The book of Proverbs names knowledge as the beginning of wisdom and understanding. Add to education the commitment to improve as a person spiritually, physically, emotionally, and socially.

Principle and education are the architects of the soul that spur us on to excellence in specific responsibilities, among them the protection of the environment.

ENVIRONMENT

"Save the Earth Day" is a national celebration founded to promote national awareness of pollution and recycling. Individuals are becoming more responsible as information and promotion of these issues flourishes. Whereas blame was once laid primarily on industry, the shift has now been changed to a shared responsibility of the populace. *The Buffalo News* dramatically described the earth's condition with this statement: "Children alive today may live to see the first man on Mars and the last elm tree in the United States."

The creation account of Genesis tells of God's tender and thoughtful plan in creating the earth for man's enjoyment. At the end of His design, He pronounced it "good." The command that follows to replenish the earth is usually applied to producing children, but we have in these days begun to understand its broader meaning. Care is to be bestowed upon vegetation to enable its renewal and upon animal life to encourage reproduction. Mankind has taken advantage of the environment for thousands of years but recently has come to understand that for every misuse, our children and future generations will suffer the consequences.

The planet known as earth is a type of Noah's Ark. It is for our protection and provision, and there will not be another given to us in this life. Described as a fragile and precious life-support system, it is the only body in our solar system known to harbor and nourish life.

Human activity and innovation in chemical production have punched a hole in the ozone layer, turned once-fertile soil into deserts, and destroyed hundreds of thousands of square miles of forest around the globe. Even Superman's cape couldn't protect against the harshness of present-day acid rain. No matter how often the younger generation (and not-so-younger) speaks of being "cool" in attitude, the greenhouse effect on the environment continues to bring about a global warming of the planet.

There is, for the first time in generations, a universal trend toward saving the environment. At an annual conference of the Group of Seven (the United States, Japan, West Germany, Britain, France, Canada, and Italy) held in Paris, environmental issues received unprecedented attention. The media named it the "environmental summit." The group pledged to work together to preserve the global environment, saying in its communiqué: "Decisive action is urgently needed to understand and protect the earth's ecological balance. We will work together to achieve the common goals of preserving a healthy and balanced global environment in order to meet shared economic and social objectives."

I agree with the prominently displayed philosophy of the Hard Rock Cafe: "Save the Planet." It will come in handy in the future!

Commitment to anything—whether educational or environmental—requires a decision toward excellence.

EXCELLENCE

To quote Paul Laxalt once again: "We must overcome the worrisome one-liners such as 'At the rate things are going, the Japanese will be making all the products, and we'll be taking in each other's laundry,' or 'All the real jobs are going overseas. All that's left for us is making hamburgers.'" Such pessimistic statements are ridiculous and small-minded.

Former Chrysler chairman Lee Iaococa spent many years in print, television, radio, and in person spreading the message that American-made automobiles were as good or better as foreign models. So fervent was he in his goal that Chrysler made a major comeback and became synonymous with quality products.

We need more publications like Ben Wattenberg's *The Good News Is That the Bad News Is Wrong*. There are enough major affirmatives occurring in our world to gain anyone's attention. It is an exciting time in which to live as we witness historic occasions firsthand such as the pulling down of the Berlin Wall, the fall of the Iron Curtain from its hinges of Communism, and the signing of a peace treaty between former bitter enemies Israel and the Palestine Liberation Organization.

There was a noticeable difference between my first trip to the Soviet Union and my last. In the latter, I enjoyed an American hamburger from McDonald's and bought a *Business Week Magazine*, both representing the epitome of capitalism and the free enterprise system. In the former, these things and others like them did not exist. Partnerships are expanding around the world—a Wendy's in Taiwan, a 7–Eleven in Singapore, Mary Kay cosmetics in Malaysia, Disneyland in Tokyo and near Paris.

No matter the accuracy of depressing statistics, you can find genuine positive signs of growth and productivity as well. And when those seem scarce, we take it as an open opportunity to rewrite facts through a commitment to excellence in goals. Pessimism thrives on despair, but passion for excellence does not even recognize it. Minimize and alter the effect of depression through a devotion to the pursuit of excellence in all areas of life. Replace the melody of mediocrity with the whistle of a winner. It is the difference between the win, the place, and the show in the race of life.

I read an inspiring plaque in the office of a friend:

Excellence can be attained if you . . .

- *Care more than others think is wise.*

- *Risk more than others think is safe.*

- *Dream more than others think is practical.*

- *Expect more than others think is possible.*

Legendary football coach Vince Lombardi defined excellence as an essential to the quality of life: "The quality of a person's life is in direct proportion to their commitment to excellence, regardless of their chosen field of endeavor." Excellence is the catalyst to tenacity and the consistent goal of finding a better way.

I have determined for myself not to be diverted by prevailing pessimism nor intimidated by the rapidly deteriorating conditions out of my control. We cannot fear failure, criticism, or costs; and most of all, we cannot lose faith in the future that God has planned for us.

Awareness does not have to breed apprehension. Analysis of the problems must not result in paralysis of potential. To Chicken Little and her modern-day companions we say, "Take another look at the sky. It's not exploding—it's expanding into untapped opportunities available for the taking." As proof of this, I offer the promise of God to every child of His:

> "For I know the thoughts that I have for you," says the LORD, "thoughts of peace and not of evil, to give you a future and a hope."
>
> Jeremiah 29:11

What an incredible truth! God Himself is thinking about *my* future. He is thinking about *your* future! Whether our successes will be chronicled in journalism is not of importance. The emphasis is on the fact that God is preparing a plan. Reflect on this . . . the Creator of the Universe is personally creating your future.

The first time I heard this verse from Jeremiah, I must admit I was overwhelmed. But then it suddenly made sense. We were created by Him, with His own hands, from His own heart. Of course He wants His personal creations to be a success. Of course He is thinking of us!

10

LIVING LIFE
UPSIDE DOWN

Some say we've risen to a new age of truth . . .
We have a program for saving the earth while unborn
    children are denied their right to birth.
One baby's blessed, another one cursed,
Well, you tell me, have we made this world better or worse
Now that the life of a tree comes first?
And you say we've risen to a new age of light,
You're telling me what used to be wrong is now right,
But I say—What if we're living life upside down?

Adapted from "Living Life Upside Down"
by Karla Worley and Gary Driskell

When an individual claims the Bible's miracles to be out-dated or "politically incorrect," the refusal to believe is usually based on the folly of scientific "miracles." Those who penned the words of the Creator would have laughed in derision at their claims. Such ridiculous theories were prevalent even in the days of the apostle Paul. He warned Timothy: "O Timothy!

Guard what was committed to your trust, avoiding the profane and idle babble and contradictions of what is falsely called knowledge" (1 Tim. 6:20). Much of what is labeled science is like a well without water, a cloud without rain, or a tree without fruit. Paul's wise words still call to us today in the following comparison to a sum deposited for which the bank is responsible and guards under lock and key for safekeeping: guard what was committed to your trust. A Greek word study of this phrase reveals a reference to a thing of value to be cared for and protected against damage or attack.

This is a fitting application when you consider that schools have committed a great robbery against the minds of youth in their denial of creation. The evident result is a generation on the brink of moral and spiritual bankruptcy.

The battles for the Bible as indisputable truth, for your mind, and for your soul are being waged on several fronts.

Perhaps never before in history has the command to "Be ready to give a defense to everyone who asks you a reason for the hope that is in you" (1 Pet. 3:15) been so imperative. This dictum is essential not only in defense of the faith but also as a divine protection against the rampant false teachings of the day. The abundance of false teachings is one of the warning signs given as the last days approach. However, simple knowledge without wisdom is folly, and so Peter also offers this beginning:

"Sanctify the Lord God in your hearts." The word *sanctify* is literally "to set apart." Greek scholar Kenneth Wuest says it is to "acknowledge that Christ alone is worthy of our worship." He is to occupy the throne of our lives as we focus our heart on worship of and obedience to Him. The end result is an adoption of the character of Christ, a powerful motivation toward service, and a strong defense against entanglement into false teachings.

A charge to "give a defense" does not indicate a mere retort. Rather we are to proclaim with eloquence and literally "talk one's self off from a charge preferred against one." In the Greek, "give an answer" was a technical legal term used in the courts to designate the work of an attorney as he presented a verbal defense of innocence for his client.

This serious term is chosen because of the holiness of the book we are to defend, namely, the Word of God. The Bible has been called a man-made narrative, full of possible inaccuracies, myths and fairy tales. The Bible claims divine authorship with more than twenty-five hundred references to it in the Old Testament alone.

The revelation of God came to man by means of inspiration, meaning "God-breathed."

> All Scripture is given by inspiration of God, and is profitable for doctrine, for reproof, for correction, for instruction in righteousness.
>
> 2 Timothy 3:16

Some will tell you the Bible is simply the work of man—it's a lie. Don't believe it.

> Knowing this first, that no prophecy of Scripture is of any private interpretation, for prophecy never came by the will of man, but holy men of God spoke as they were moved by the Holy Spirit.
>
> 2 Peter 1:20

Man could not have produced such a work without the Holy Spirit. The term *moved* is an interesting picture in the original Greek language. It was used to describe a sailing vessel, carried along or "moved" by the winds.

Do not be led astray by what many say is "partial inspiration." *All Scripture* includes Genesis through Revelation—every word is truth. It has become fashionable in many academic settings to ridicule the historical accuracy of the accounts of Adam and Eve, Noah, Jonah, and other Old Testament personalities. Jesus Himself authenticated the Old Testament by quoting from it; it anticipated the New Testament with many prophecies and teachings. He protected the authenticity by reminding us "till heaven and earth pass away, one jot or one tittle will by no means pass from the law till all is fulfilled" (Matt. 5:18).

Think about it: A "jot" is the smallest character in the Hebrew alphabet, less than half the size of any other character in the list. The "tittle" is a little horn-shaped mark used by the ancient Hebrews to mark consonants. This verse is a strong affirmation of the divine authority of the entire Word of God.

This doctrine of inspiration is at the very foundation of all that we believe. In fact, any other doctrine is folly without the veracity of it. This issue must once and for all be settled in our own minds and hearts lest we become mediocre in our commitment to Christ. The challenges to your faith have only just begun. You have already faced the challenge of evolution theory in high school, but the battle will intensify in college. You are about to enter a new academic arena of such ferocious debate that many have been destroyed by it.

Author Samuel Blumenfield aptly titled his work *Who Killed Excellence?* when he wrote about modern education. He answered the question of his title in this way: "Behavioral psychology did because it is based on a lie, that man is simply an animal without a mind or a soul, and he can be taught as an animal. That concept is based on even a greater lie; that there is no God, no Creator. And so the future of American education rests on the resolution of profoundly philosophical questions."

EVOLUTION

Evolution is the mother of all skepticism. There will be those who will laugh in disbelief as you quote the simple, powerful truth of Genesis 1:1—"In the beginning God created the heavens and the earth." It is understandable that you have an interest in the origin of the universe and of life itself. Certainly the debate between evolution and creation is one of the most controversial subjects today. Science must answer the questions "From where?" and "How?" Since science is based on cause-and-effect reasoning, it is inevitable that we ponder the first cause. A proper understanding of where we came from will shape our self-image and our long-range goals. What we believe about our origin shapes our belief about our destiny.

There are fundamentally only two explanations for the obvious fact that man is unique among creatures and distinct from animal life. You must choose either the explanation found in the first and second chapters of the book of Genesis, that man is a supernatural creation, or the evolutionary theory that man is the product of a mechanistic and impersonal universe. Has God ordained the plan in which all things work together, or have random change and chance events brought this about? The choice is between the God of the Bible and the theory that began with Charles Darwin.

Genesis is the first book of the Bible, and it is the book of beginnings. It tells of the origin of the universe, the origin of life, and the origin of man. It shows that man is the direct, complete, supernatural creation of a personal, loving Creator. Man also has a given purpose in life, under God.

> Then God said, "Let Us make man in Our image, according to Our likeness; let them have dominion over the fish of the sea, over the birds of the air, and over the cattle, over all the earth and over every creeping thing that creeps on the earth." So God created man in His own image; in the image of God He created him; male and female He created them. Then God blessed them, and God said to them "Be fruitful and multiply; fill the earth and subdue it; have dominion over the fish of the sea, over the birds of the air, and over every living thing that moves on the earth."
>
> Genesis 1:26–28

Man's nature may be described as a composite. Man is usually referred to as a union of spirit, soul, and body (1 Thess. 5:23). Man is a unity, each part of which interacts with the others

(Matt. 26:41; Heb. 4:12; 1 Pet. 2:11). It is the spirituality of man that separates him from the animal kingdom and makes it possible for him to be God-conscious. He can sense the presence and love of God, enjoy communion with God, and possesses a conscience to discern right from wrong. The biblical record states that God did not create man as a savage, but that He created him complete and full-grown, with all of his faculties. Immediately after his creation, the intelligent Adam named all beasts and birds of the earth.

What is meant by the "image" of God (Gen. 1:27)? This image does not refer to His physical nature, for "God is Spirit" (John 4:24), and "a spirit does not have flesh and bones" (Luke 24:39). The image and likeness consist of spiritual nature (Gen. 1:26). This spiritual nature endowed man with the power of choice, making Adam a free moral agent with moral, emotional, and spiritual capabilities.

Man was the crowning act of earthly creation, perfect in intellectual life and moral life. His physical perfection was the reflection of his spiritual quality. As the apex of creation, Adam had special self-awareness, which allowed him to think, dream, reflect, and react in a unique way. He was made in the image and likeness of God.

Evolution is a theory, not a scientific fact. The dictionary defines the word *theory* as "doctrine, an admitted guess or supposition." If you were to ask an evolutionist about the origin, nature, and purpose of man, he would reply that man evolved from the lower animals by a process of natural selection. He would say that man is only another member of the animal order, as is apparent by comparing his skeletal structure and vital organs with those of other animals. He would insist that there is no scientific evidence that man possesses a soul; therefore, upon death, a person must cease to exist.

In considering evolution, you should realize that never has any system of thought been built upon so many statements prefaced by words like "perhaps," "probably," "possibly," "it may be," "it seems to be," "it must be," "it could have been," and "quite conceivable." If you read *The Origin of the Species* by

Charles Darwin, you will count several hundred such statements of opinion. But consider these statements:

1. Man is distinct from beasts. In blood, in bone, in flesh, cells, mind, soul, and spirit, humankind is unique.

2. Only man has a thumb that enables him to handle tools and instruments.

3. Man walks erect. There is no other anthropoid that does so.

4. Man has a radically superior mentality. Try teaching evolution to a monkey, or astronomy to an eagle, or geology to a rock badger, or theology to a porpoise. Yet even the most primitive Aborigines of Australia can learn all four.

5. Darwin taught that somewhere there came into existence a speck (cell) of protoplasm, and that man evolved from that speck through innumerable transitional forms—although there are no fossil remains of transitional forms or "links" between species of animal life. Some scientists today tell us that the earth was covered with poisonous gases. Then "possibly" a bolt of lightning or explosion made a combination of chemicals that "possibly" formed our oceans, and that "possibly" an amino acid resulted, which then evolved into a tiny cell that was invisible to the naked eye. Through generations, from that single cell, there evolved all the forms of life in the plant and animal world, they say.

6. Of course the main question remains unanswered. Where did the first cell of protoplasm come from? And where did the water to nurture it come from? The Latin proverb applies: "Out of nothing comes nothing."

Time magazine's feature story on October 11, 1993, afforded the scientific community a platform on which to parade its theories. I refer to a well-written article by Madeline Nash, which gave a potpourri of evolution theories for consideration.

The first I have dubbed "Darwin's Warm Little Pond of Broth." Charles Darwin imagined (noticed I didn't say proved) that the birthplace of life contained a rich broth of organic chemicals. Over eons of time, he conjectured, they gradually assembled themselves into primitive organisms.

Another theory was that of hydrothermal vents: the eerie environs of undersea geysers offer a stygian (musky or gloomy) alternative to Darwin's sunlit pond. Near the scalding steamers supposedly lived some of earth's most archaic creatures.

In lane number three is the bubbles theory: Foam in the sea *could have* provided another breeding place by collecting a concentration of many materials essential to life, including molecules forming cell-like membranes.

Let me not forget to mention the hypothetical fiery cradle theory: The first creatures arose more than 3.5 billion years ago while the earth was still a volcanic cauldron.

Let me get this straight: millions of different species of animals—including more than 800,000 different kinds of insects, 30,000 varieties of fish, 9,000 types of birds, 6,000 sorts of reptiles, 2,000 forms of amphibians, and 5,000 categories of mammals—leapt from an isolated form struggling in primordial soup.

Hmmm, as Wayne said to Garth—"That *could* happen. Yeah, right." It takes far more faith to believe explanations such as these than it does to believe "Thus saith the Lord." Every one of the theories requires a miracle greater than biblical creation! It would be like an explosion of a printing shop resulting in *Webster's New Collegiate Dictionary.*

It is unlikely that life and the universe evolved by *chance.* God is still asking today, "Where were *you* when I laid the foundations of the earth?" (Job 38:4; John 1:1–4; Col. 1:16)

ABORTION

Seeing man as an animal has given way to the present-day climate of society in which abortion is both tolerated and encouraged. As we have already seen, the Bible clearly reveals the plan of God in creation. Numerous verses teach us that the developing child is the expression of God's greatest earthly creation, namely the human being. When a woman is pregnant, God Himself is forming a child within her.

> For You formed my inward parts;
> You covered me in my mother's womb.
> I will praise You, for I am fearfully and wonderfully
>   made;
> Marvelous are Your works,
> And that my soul knows very well.
>   Psalm 139:13–14

God's direct address to not only Jeremiah's creation but also the individual plan chosen for his life is evidence of the sanctity of an unborn child:

> Before I formed you in the womb I knew you;
> Before you were born I sanctified you;
> I ordained you a prophet to the nations.
>   Jeremiah 1:5

When does life begin? According to Christian consensus, life begins at "quickening," or conception. It is a biological fact that when the union of the sperm and the egg occurs, the twenty-three chromosomes of each are brought together into one cell, making up forty-six chromosomes. At that moment one cell has all the DNA (the whole genetic determinate of our height, color of hair and eyes, and other characteristics) that will, if not interrupted, form a human being. The child needs only food and time to grow into an adult human. As early as eighteen days following conception the human heart begins to beat, long before the mother is sure of her pregnancy. At six weeks brain waves can be recorded. By the ninth and tenth weeks, the thyroid and adrenal glands begin to function. The baby can swallow and move the tongue. Even the sex hormones are present. By the twelfth and thirteenth weeks the baby has fingernails, sucks the thumb, and reacts to pain. Perfectly formed fingerprints exist that will distinguish the child as a separate entity for the rest of life.

Since January 22, 1973, when the Supreme Court upheld the legalization of abortion, there have been more than twenty million abortions in this country alone. Reports indicate approximately one and one-half million abortions are performed every year, about four thousand per day. The most common surgical procedure in the United States used to be tonsillectomy. Today, it is the abortion.

From a legal standpoint, the worse decision ever rendered by the United States Supreme Court to date may have been the Roe-versus-Wade decision, which legalized the murder of millions of unborn babies. More babies have died through abortion than all the soldiers ever killed in our major wars. Ironically, laws have been established to protect children from abuse, abandonment, and withholding of necessary medical treatment.

This great country has laws to conserve eagle eggs, baby whales, and a host of other creatures. Our children have witnessed the nation's show of concern for rescuing California gray whales trapped in ice off of Point Barrow, Alaska. Support and assistance flooded in from several countries in this endeavor, and both national and international media covered the ordeal. But nothing is in place to protect the unborn child from utter and complete destruction save the decision of a mother.

The unborn child is called a fetus, not a person. No one wants to discuss the Latin meaning of *fetus,* which is literally "unborn child." Abortion ends with a dead baby, a childless mother, and a long and painful memory. Fortunately, God's grace is greater than our sin, and we can receive healing of the memories for the asking.

The great debate over when life begins has encouraged confusion over the decision to legalize euthanasia and suicide. Are you beginning to see how the very core of God's truths are being attacked? In a domino effect, each profoundly impacts the other.

EUTHANASIA/SUICIDE

One of the most tragic trends of the nineties is self-induced euthanasia. Euthanasia was called by *Time* magazine "an unfortunate consequence of modern medicine's ability to keep people alive in a state of semi-death." The case for the right to suicide has been glorified by primarily two people: Dr. Jack Kevorkian, called by the media "Dr. Death," and Derek Humphrey, the author of *Final Exit*.

Kevorkian has become a national news story with his machines developed specifically to assist people in taking their own life. Humphrey's book is intended as a "how-to" manual in which he casually recommends cyanide, gas from an oven, hangings, and shootings.

The Bible teaches that suicide is a sin against God. Very simply, God commands "You shall not murder" (Exod. 20:13). Suicide is just that—murdering yourself. Although it is a sin, it is one that God can and does forgive. Christ died for every sin and forgives every sin but one, that is, not believing in and accepting what Christ did for you on the cross and in His resurrection. Still, suicide is a violation of God's law.

The Lord described His creation as, "Indeed it was very good" (Gen. 1:31). Jesus said of life, "I have come that they may have life, and that they may have it more abundantly" (John 10:10). To commit suicide is to reject all of the joy and goodness of life that God promises us.

Even so, eternal life in heaven is based on our personal relationship with God Himself, not on the manner in which we die.

If you have a friend or loved one who has committed suicide, do not let that last irrational act be the one you dwell on. All of the happiness and goodness offered to you and others should not be forgotten. Some people are not able to cope as well with the pressures of life. We need to react in love rather than in condemnation.

Few circumstances can duplicate the degree of intense pain that suicide produces. Loved ones left behind struggle to make sense of the tragedy. There is no such thing as a good reason to commit suicide, but here are some of the rationales given by those who have attempted to do so.

- *Inescapable problems*—A sense of hopelessness prevails because there seems to be no way out (for example—family problems, social relationships, loss of job, poor school grades).

- *To "get even"*—Because feelings have been hurt, the offended one will use suicide to lash out in a vengeful attitude, hoping to cause a sense of guilt in the survivors.

- *To gain attention*—Suicide is a cry for attention, hoping for failure in the attempt, hoping for lavish attention afterward.

- *To join deceased loved ones*—This is particularly true in the case of a mother, father, or mate passing away.

- *To avoid consequences*—This can involve financial indebtedness, punishment by law for committing a crime, or an illegitimate pregnancy.

- *To pledge love*—In the case of a broken relationship, either forced by parents or by one of the partners, it is a statement of "I can't live without you," a playback of the Romeo and Juliet story.

Keep in mind that most who attempt suicide do not really want to die. They want help and direction. If you or a friend is having thoughts of suicide, you should immediately seek the counsel of your parents, pastor, youth worker, or church leader for help in finding joy and purpose in living. It is most important that these feelings be talked out. Everyone faces pressures in life. You are not alone. Help is available, and you should not be afraid or ashamed to seek it.

Don't avoid your responsibility to saying yes to God's best by copping out with "I just can't handle it!" God promises you can overcome anything through His help.

> No temptation has overtaken you except such as is common to man; but God is faithful, who will not allow you to be tempted beyond what you are able, but with the temptation will also make the way of escape, that you may be able to bear it.
>
> 1 Corinthians 10:13

Depend fully on God's deep love for you and allow Him to lead you through every problem of life.

BIOETHICS/GENETIC ENGINEERING

These are perhaps the most troubling concerns of all because they are double-edged in their consequence. On one hand, future generations will greatly benefit from their medical breakthroughs. On the other, there is extreme potential for harm, particularly in light of man's propensity for "playing God."

Albert Einstein, who developed the special and general theory of relativity, was sensitive to man's need for restraint. His equation of $E=mc^2$ led to nuclear fission and, hence, the atomic bomb. *The Dictionary of Cultural Literacy* states Einstein believed strongly in the regularity of nature. He said, "God does not play dice with the universe. God is subtle, but not malicious."

It is imperative to distinguish between the theory of relativity in which the laws of nature are constant in all the universe and the philosophical doctrine of relativity, which holds that there are no absolute truths. The similarity in names is confusing both to the scientist as well as the student.

We who have been converted through the words of the Bible are exhorted to present a verbal defense, proving false every charge against the standards set forth by God in His Word. We are to continually contend for the faith once and for all delivered to the saints against those "who exchanged the truth of God for the lie, and worshiped and served the creature rather than the Creator, who is blessed forever. Amen" (Rom. 1:25).

In these confusing times, there are those who conveniently forget the intervention of God from creation to the flood to the incarnation "when God became flesh and blood and moved into the neighborhood" (John 1:14, from *The Message*). If I do not maintain God in my thoughts, then I forget also that He invaded time and space for me. He came looking for Adam in the Garden, and He is looking for you. Moral confusion always leads to mental confusion.

"They pretended to know it all, but were illiterate regarding life. They traded the glory of God Who holds the world in His hands for cheap figurines you can buy at any roadside stand" (Rom. 1:22–23, *The Message*). The result has been a spiritual and moral Chernobyl, where experts deny any connection but the damage is extensive.

Physical and historical proof of the gospel miracles, including the resurrection of Christ, fulfilled prophecies, and transformed lives of believers are all proof positive of the reality of God and His power. We must develop the habit of looking at the issues of life solely from God's point of view.

11

HOW TO BE
FIVE-FOOT-NINE
IN A NINE-FOOT
WORLD

It has been called "the great American dream" to make a mark in society, become successful, accomplish the impossible, and thereby to attain contentment and happiness. The spring of hope eternal wells within the heart of the young man or woman facing a world of possibilities for tomorrow. With exuberance and optimism, the graduate begins the journey not realizing that the snares of diverse enemies lie in wait. Your generation believes it is invulnerable and that the "good life" will just naturally follow. Then the robber comes to steal the dream, the critic assaults in an effort to discourage, and the disappointments slow the quest for excellence into a stroll of mediocrity. What begins as the drive to achieve can evolve into a stalled hope.

The psalmist David was familiar with such foes. As a shepherd boy he faced the lion and the bear and even a giant named Goliath. David may have been "five-foot-nine in a nine-foot world," as my good friend Ike Reighard says, but the immensity of his courage gave him victory over life's difficulties. He did not volunteer to battle this champion of war because Goliath shamed his country or his family, but because Goliath disregarded the living God of Israel. David was motivated and enabled through the power of righteous anger.

Let's visit the battlefield of the Israelites and their perennial and perpetual enemy, the Philistines. After days of a seesaw battle, a standoff occurs: "The Philistines stood on a mountain on one side, and Israel stood on a mountain on the other side, with a valley between them" (1 Sam. 17:3). As Israel huddles together in strategic planning, a mountain of a man approaches the camp. Fear assaults the heart of every man as they behold this nine-foot hulk of a man standing before them. With arms as big as the cedars of Lebanon, hands like the talons of an eagle, eyes as intense as bolts of lightning, and a voice of clapping thunder, he booms forth a challenge: "Choose a man for yourselves, and let him come down to me. If he is able to fight with me and kill me, then we will be your servants. But if I prevail against him and kill him, then you shall be our servants and serve us" (1 Sam. 17:8–9).

For forty days he dared them to fight him until finally the army of Israel withdrew in trepidation. This giant was the "undisputed heavyweight champion of the world" when it came to battle, and no one was brave enough to come forward and accept the dare. No one, that is, but young, inexperienced, hopeful, full-of-faith David.

Bringing food to his elder brothers serving in the army, the young shepherd boy, probably about your age, now enters the scene. The thundering taunts of the giant stir his blood, and he immediately volunteers to take on the giant antagonist. Family, friends, and fellow Israelites are unanimous in their criticism and sarcasm of David. He rebukes them with the cry: "Is there not a cause?" In the name of the Lord, David overcomes the powerful enemy with a heart of faith, a sure commitment of purpose, and one smooth stone. And because Goliath was but one of the many giants in the land, David, thinking ahead, took along four extra stones just in case any brothers showed up!

In every life, there are "giants" blocking the path to success, to improvement, to achievement of goals and dreams. They will come defying the truth and power of the living God as they jeer at and mock the generation of tomorrow. These may be the wrong group of friends, depression, a lack of belief in yourself, or an overwhelming disappointment. David's quest offers us some spiritual lessons on standing tall against the obstacles before us.

A CAUSE WORTH FIGHTING FOR

First and foremost, we see David's energy was directed into a *cause worth fighting for.* The secret of David's courage is seen in his commitment to the cause. Being ready to die for the sake of His God put steel into the backbone of a young man while the strong men around him trembled. His experience seemed of little consequence to others, yet God chose to bless his faithfulness in the small things as preparation for a mighty future. Consider David in the pasture or standing by a campfire. I believe it was during the everyday tasks of life that David resolved to follow the Lord *no matter what.* What you must understand is that David did not prepare *after* the decision to fight Goliath— he had been preparing all his life. Although he didn't realize it then, David would become one of the greatest generals, kings, and musicians to ever be recorded in history.

Ecclesiastes 12:1 exhorts us to "Remember now your Creator in the days of your youth." *Now* is the time—every day—as you go through every situation, decision, and circumstance. If you haven't been living a life of faith in Christ, don't read another word until you stop and pray a simple prayer of surrender: "Lord, I commit my heart totally to you." As a young man of seventeen I first prayed that prayer in need of salvation and since then have prayed it many times in my life in a time of re-commitment to God's will for me.

CHARACTER WORTH LIVING BY

Even as a young man, David displayed *character worth living by.* My favorite definition of character is "doing what is right on purpose." A firm conviction in right living involves *making decisions in advance and sticking to them.* When you have character, you win the battle even when you fight alone as David did when he killed the lion and the bear in the field. Character moved David to humbly and faithfully choose serving others. Notice he was bringing food to his brothers—just running errands for the family without whining or complaining—when his historic, life-changing opportunity came. Tomorrow's leaders are being formed today and every day.

What we do with our private time will eventually give birth to our public life. For David, he served others, as we mentioned. He was faithful to the task, no matter the size. He practiced playing the harp with the intent of giving praise to God. He made excellent use of his discretionary time, and he was promoted by the Lord in reward.

A CALCULATION WORTH BELIEVING IN

Though he walked with the Lord in His heart, the young shepherd boy had no clue of his future until that fateful day. Presented with the challenge, he made a *calculation worth believing in.* One slingshot, five smooth stones—was he thinking ahead to Goliath's four sons (2 Sam. 21:22) or preparing himself for the possibility of other enemies lurking in wait? He made this calculation: the opponent's resources were limited—"You come to me with a sword, with a spear, and with a javelin" (1 Sam. 17:45a). His own resources were unlimited: "But I come to you in the name of the LORD" (1 Sam. 17:45b). Wow! Talk about an adventure movie!

Fully reflect on the battle before you and count the cost of the victory. Calculate:

1. What or who you are up against.

2. What or who your resources are.

3. What pitfalls lurk in the background.

A CONSCIOUSNESS WORTH TRUSTING IN

David's calculations were successful because he had a consciousness *worth trusting in.* One of the secrets to success is to first discover the truth of God and then to discover your own being. David knew who he was *not.* He was not Saul (1 Sam. 17:38–39). The armor given to him had not been tested. It simply was not suitable for him no matter how well-tailored for others. In fact, to rely on it would have resulted in sure defeat.

David's strong self-image was derived from his faith in God. Even as he listed his accomplishments, he spoke of the Lord. In my own young life, I struggled for many years with feelings of inadequacy, inferiority, and, frankly, insignificance. As a new Christian someone read me this verse, and I have never been the same: "If God is for us, who can be against us?" (Rom. 8:31b).

Shortly thereafter I discovered Philippians 4:13: "I can do all things through Christ who strengthens me." Slowly, but surely, I began to understand the source of my self-image as God's love for me and my faith in Him.

Tuned into the heart of God, confident in himself, David was able to ignore the unspiritual advice of the king and trust in his own beliefs. Notice the criticism heaped upon the lad, yet he did not waver and walked even "where angels fear to tread."

THREE TYPES OF PEOPLE

Three types of people emerge from this narrative.

The Losers. There were many of these. They worried, discussed, complained, criticized, but never accomplished a thing or made one positive contribution. The older brother of David jeered "What are you doing here?" He then turned to the crowd and enticed them to criticize. I hesitate to label anyone a "loser," but I know in every group there will be those whose only sure belief is failure in a given situation.

The Leaners. These gathered at the nearby well to enjoy the comfort of one another's cowardice. If you hang out with cowards, no one will actually accuse you of being one because in doing so they label themselves. Psychologists call it "the safety of the herd." A leaner holds up a wet finger to determine which way the wind of public opinion is blowing that day. A leaner would probably hold a secret ballot to select the one to fight the giant.

The Leaders. From the madness of the mob emerged one lone figure—David, the leader. He has been called the greatest leader in the Old Testament. Surveying the situation, he steps forward and proclaims, "Here I am. I will do it." The leader stands up, accepts the challenge, verbalizes his decision, and moves ahead.

If, after reading this, you are still thinking "I don't think I've got what it takes," read on:

> But the LORD said to Samuel, "Do not look at his appearance or at his physical stature, because I have refused him. For the LORD does not see as man sees; for man looks at the outward appearance, but the LORD looks at the heart."
>
> 1 Samuel 16:7

After all of the preparing and the deciding, affirm yourself. Don't be afraid of the giants awaiting you. Like Goliath they can be toppled. *You can* be the victor in the name of the Lord!

12

WHEN YOU FEEL LIKE QUITTING—DON'T!

Pursued by the powerful Egyptian army, the children of Israel come face-to-face with the mammoth Red Sea. Many murmured, "Let's go back even if it's to bondage." A ridiculous choice, of course. Moses proclaimed, "Stand still and wait on the Lord." This seems like an option of faith until you hear the command of God in response to the situation: "Go forward!" "Forward by faith" became the cry of the children of Israel as they watched the Red Sea miraculously part.

These same choices await every young man and woman today. Standing on the threshold of your "Promised Land," you will be tempted to give up (go back) or put off the difficult (stand still); or you will be motivated to go forward. I remember my move from Florida to South Carolina, where I enrolled in Charleston Southern University. Leaving behind family, friends, and a secure career was a difficult decision, but the excitement of new opportunities ahead bolstered my courage.

Making my way to the first day on a job, the joy of anticipation quickly faded into despair. The coveted position as associate pastor was awarded to a young man with more education and experience. My dream was dismissed with a simple "I'm sorry." Diane and I struggled for several months as we searched for housing and employment—each time coming up empty-handed. Discouragement began to overwhelm me, and I wondered if I had missed God's will. About that time, I was invited to return to Florida in the same position but at a better salary. Family and friends encouraged me to return, and at times, I felt it was just too difficult to stay and wait for the unknown. My wife and I struggled with the decision to go back or move forward in spite of the adverse circumstances.

I know how it feels to want to quit or to take the easier road of life. In my case, there was nothing wrong with the easier road. It was a good road, but it represented a "standstill" in my future. It simply was not the *best* choice. As it turned out, I received a wonderful position at a church in Charleston. It didn't begin with as much prestige, but it later developed into opportunities and relationships that I still benefit from today.

The winner's circle is full of great people, but practically void of those who made it without a struggle. The strenuous climb to the top of the goal is what makes the win a joyous one. When you've done all you can, you're tired, embarrassed, discouraged, and ready to quit. But there are many things you can do.

1. DON'T QUIT! Endure, persevere, and stay strong. As Franklin D. Roosevelt once said, "When you get to the end of your rope, tie a knot in it and hang on!" Make the decision, once and for all, to *continue* ahead. As long as any doubt remains in your heart, the determination to go forward cannot overcome the discouragement.

2. EXAMINE THE WORK YOU HAVE ALREADY DONE. Former distance runner and Olympic gold medalist Frank Shorter reviewed the grueling hours of training and concluded, "I didn't want to quit and say for the rest of my life, 'Well,

maybe I *could* have been . . .'" Have you come this far only to give up now? NO, NO, of course not!

> *I press toward the goal for the prize of*
> *the upward call of God in Christ Jesus.*
>
> Philippians 3:14

3. COUNT YOUR BLESSINGS: The Puritans lived by this creed: "Before making a request to God, first pay rent by offering to Him thanksgiving for His previous blessings." In nineties vernacular we would say, "Put some gratitude into your attitude."

   Helen Keller gave this secret of a joyful life in her book, *The Story of My Life*: "Three things I thank God for every day of my life—that He has granted me knowledge of His works; that He has set in my darkness the lamp of faith; and deepest thanks that I have another life to look forward to—a life of joy, flowers, heavenly songs, and the light of His glory."

   Whenever I am discouraged, I begin to list anything and everything good and positive. Weighing the blessings of life always gives me confidence and results in a realignment of priorities.

> *Be anxious for nothing, but in everything by*
> *prayer and supplication, with thanksgiving,*
> *let your requests be made known to God;*
> *and the peace of God, which surpasses all*
> *understanding, will guard your hearts*
> *and minds through Christ Jesus.*
>
> Philippians 4:6–7

4. TURN WEAKNESS INTO STRENGTH. Major League Baseball Hall of Famer Babe Ruth knew this principle well. He gave this advice to young "wanna-be" ballplayers: "A part of control is learning to correct your weaknesses. The person doesn't live who was born with everything. Sometimes he has one weak point; generally, he has several. The first thing is to know your faults and then take on a systematic plan of correcting them. You know the old saying about a chain being only as strong as its weakest link. The same can be said in the chain of skills a man forges."

Paul the apostle wrote about praying on several occasions for his physical problems. When the healing did not take place, he began to understand God's hand in infirmities:

> *And He said to me, "My grace is sufficient for you, for My strength is made perfect in weakness." Therefore most gladly I will rather boast in my infirmities, that the power of Christ may rest upon me. Therefore I take pleasure in infirmities, in reproaches, in needs, in persecutions, in distresses, for Christ's sake. For when I am weak, then I am strong.*
> 2 Corinthians 12:9–10

Examine your weaknesses. The struggles they produce are actually your strengthening exercises. These spiritual and emotional aerobics are the keys to endurance in crossing the finish line to goals and dreams.

5. ACCEPT RESPONSIBILITY FOR YOUR MISTAKES. There will never be improvement until

error is evaluated. Blaming others or circumstances leaves you trudging hopelessly in failure.

> *Whoever loves instruction loves knowledge,*
> *But he who hates correction is stupid.*
>
> Proverbs 12:1

This can be your greatest source of knowledge—to learn the best way by watching the effect of doing it the wrong way. It is impossible to live without making a mistake. Whether the error constitutes failure or wisdom depends on your response to it. While others dreamed of building a better car, Henry Ford did it because he believed "failure is only the opportunity to begin again more intelligently."

6. PLAN NEW GOALS. At this point in your life, you may be thinking, "Why plan new goals? I can't even keep up with what I'm working on right now!" Whether you are on your way to college, the military, vocational training, or a new career, you will daily be presented with goals others have set for you. Don't be frustrated by the demand of deadlines, time limits, corrections, or quotas. Instead, use these pressures to further your sense of accomplishment. The new goals will probably be a more productive means to meet the demands at hand. Success is never achieved by accident; it is carefully planned, calculated, and striven for.

7. REDIRECT YOUR THINKING. The larger the obstacle looms before you, the more important this step becomes in your life. If your tenacity is sure but you still feel uneasy, perhaps it is the method

or motive that is in need of evaluation. The establishment of a new perspective can be like a vitamin to the emotions. Former Dallas Cowboys manager Tex Schramm used to tell players, "Never let yesterday take up too much of today."

It is clearly the will of God for us to achieve great things and stand as a positive testimony to the world. By doing so we become a virtual reality of Scripture:

> *I can do all things through Christ*
> *who strengthens me.*
>
> Philippians 4:13

Cellular phones are commonplace today and even wireless facsimile is a reality, but can you imagine what people thought when Alexander Graham Bell first presented the idea of voices traveling over wires? He was scorned by many as a ridiculous fool. Indeed, several of his initial attempts were failures. Fortunately for us, he didn't quit, and today we benefit greatly from his endurance.

When the world seems to surround you with negative thoughts and jeers, turn to the Lord for a new outlook.

> *Often we stare so hard and long at the closed door*
> *that we miss the gentle breeze of opportunity*
> *flowing through the open window beside it.*

And do not be conformed to this world, but be transformed by the renewing of your mind, that you may prove what is that good and acceptable and perfect will of God (Rom. 12:2).

8. TAKE THE DAYS IN SHORT BITES. The vastness of a project can be overwhelming. The steps to the goal seem to flow together like a long, winding river of sweat and tears. "I can't do it" lurks in the back of the mind ready to spring forth at any moment. This is the time to take the big picture and break it into manageable parts. At the end of each day, survey your work and compliment yourself on a job well done. In this way you enjoy the project and celebrate success all along the way instead of only at the end.

Years ago, I traveled on a mission trip to India. Whenever a difficulty would arise, the pastor would say to me "Even an elephant can be eaten one bite at a time." I've never forgotten the vivid illustration of realizing a goal through a step-by-step plan. Short-term goals enable the monitoring of progress. When NASA launches a rocket, it follows a series of checkpoints before finally proclaiming, "It's a go!" The same is true of sailing a boat or piloting a plane. Realizing environmental forces can sabotage even carefully laid plans, the captain verifies directions and studies maps along the way in a concentrated effort to arrive at the correct destination.

Arriving at the final goal involves three rules:

1. Know the exact location of your start.
2. Be sure of your destination.
3. Make adjustments and corrections to ensure progress.

We forget that most time pressures are self-imposed. *We* chose the time frame, the goal, the idea, the method. Be willing to "roll with it." Be realistic about the possibilities and take snapshots of accomplishments while you are waiting for the finished portrait. Think in terms of day-by-day accomplishments.

9. PUT TIME LIMITS ON YOUR MOODS. Defeats are real, but they don't have to dominate. Emotions cannot be denied, but they can be managed. Never make an important decision when you are tired or depressed. Study your pattern of moodiness and try to discover the common catalyst. Some moods are physically related while others are purely emotional. Of course, the spiritual part of you has a great deal to do with how you act and react. Investigate every area in an attempt to control rather than be controlled by circumstances and feelings. Happiness is a choice.

I often refer to Abraham Lincoln as the "Prince of Recovery." Look at this list:

1831	Failed in business
1832	Defeated for Legislature
1833	Second failure in business
1836	Suffered nervous breakdown
1838	Defeated for Speaker
1840	Defeated for elector
1843	Defeated for Congress
1848	Defeated for Congress
1855	Defeated for Senate
1856	Defeated for Vice President
1860	WON THE PRESIDENCY

Wouldn't you think embarrassment alone would be enough to curtail Lincoln from trying again?

When I look at this list I see not defeats, but an education. For twenty-three years Lincoln went to the School of Reaching for the Goal. The preparation and experience helped to mold the character of America's most well known and remembered President. He allowed us an intimate peek into the source of his tenacity when after a Senate race he spoke these words:

> The path was worn and slippery. My foot slipped from under me, knocking the other out of the way. But I recovered and said to myself, "It's a slip and not a fall."

10. SEEK GODLY COUNSEL. More plans, dreams, and hopes have been dashed by good intentions than any other factor. Well-meaning family and friends can be sincere in their advice yet sincerely wrong in their opinion. One rule remains steadfast through the ages: The will of God will never be contrary to the Word of God. Let this be the first measurement of every piece of counsel offered and then ignore or listen on that basis.

    Never waste precious time or energy debating what is clearly defined in the Bible. To do so would be flirtation with the danger of temptation to sin. You will only find yourself trying to alter Scripture to fit your desires and later regret it.

    Choosing godly advice begins with choosing godly associates and leadership. Ask two questions about a person:

    1. Can I agree completely with his or her values?

    2. Does he or she "walk the talk"?

While you may have acquaintances from a variety of walks of life and backgrounds, your companions or close friends should share your convictions. Have a multitude of friends; solicit advice from very few.

Perhaps you need a word of encouragement or to be listened to. Never be afraid to ask for help or to share your doubts with a prayer partner. There is a tendency to withdraw during depression, but fight it and do the opposite. Attend festive social activities, enrich friendships, get up and try new hobbies.

Two-time Olympic gold medalist/pole vaulter Bob Richards believes in drawing from the greatness all around us: "It's easy to be great because great people will help you. Great people will share; great people will tell you their secrets. Look for them, call them on the phone, or buy their books. Go where they are, get around them, talk to them. It is easy to be great when you get around great people."

11. EXAMINE PRIORITIES. Productive moments are piddled away as worry and despair take over the energy level. If the same amount of time and energy spent on worrying about a problem was used to work toward a solution, there would be a great deal more success.

I once watched NBA Maverick's player Derek Harper dribble the final six seconds off the clock because he thought his team was one up. In actuality, the game was tied and the Mavericks ended up losing in overtime.

Dribble, dribble, dribble go the minutes, the hours, the days, the years of our lives.

And you never can tell how close you are,
It may be near when it seems afar.

Jill Wolf
From *Don't Quit*

Keep your eyes open, your heart pumping, your brain charged up. Keep on keeping on until the goal is met and God's will is fulfilled. Finish what you start—"almost" just ain't good enough!

13

THE GRASSHOPPER SYNDROME

Moses commanded thirteen men to go see what the Promised Land was like (Numbers 13–14). For forty days they spied on the Promised Land and its inhabitants. They departed with the same instructions, but they returned with conflicting accounts. How could this happen?

Note that twelve of the men were each from a different tribe, thus each was from a different background. Each man reported not only what *was*, but also his *opinion* of what was. Moses did not ask, "Should we obey God and take the land?" Yet they reacted immediately with negative complaints.

Joshua and Caleb carried in proof of the land's bounty. The grapes were so heavy that one branch had to be carried "between two of them on a pole." Here is a summary of the attitudes of the *followers*:

- *The "I'm scared, let's not try it" attitude:* "It truly flows with milk and honey. . . . Nevertheless the people who dwell in the land are strong; the cities are fortified and very large" (Num. 13:27–28).

- *The "I already know I can't do it" viewpoint.* "We are not able to go up against the people, for they are stronger than we" (Num. 13:31).

- *The grasshopper syndrome:* "We saw the giants . . . and we were like grasshoppers in our own sight" (Num. 13:33).

But here is what the *leaders* had to say:

- *The heart of vision.* "Let us go up at once and take possession, for we are well able to overcome it" (Num. 13:30).

- *The heart of faith:* "If the LORD delights in us, then He will bring us into this land and give it to us, a land that flows with milk and honey" (Num. 14:8).

After these controversial summations were presented to the people, which attitude do you suppose they adopted? The negative or the positive? You guessed it! The negative is just so much easier to accept.

- *First they cried, though there was nothing yet to cry about.* "So all the congregation lifted up their voices and cried, and the people wept that night" (Num. 14:1).

- *Next they complained.* "If only we had died in Egypt! Or if only we had died in this wilderness" (Num. 14:2).

- *This led to imagining the worst possible scenario.* "Why has the LORD brought us to this land to fall by the sword, that our wives and children should become victims?" (Num. 14:3a).

- *Finally, they just gave up.* "Would it not be better for us to return to Egypt?" (Num. 14:3b).

What a bunch of whining cowards! God had already delivered them from bondage and then saved their lives through 100 percent, grade-A miracles. How quickly they forgot! All they could see was their own small abilities, and so they called themselves grasshoppers—just helpless insects.

The giants they feared were not the ones destroying their hopes. In truth they were the giants of *selfishness* and *poor self-image*. These qualities lived within their own hearts and kept them from entering into God's promise of abundance. These same powerful mammoths still control the hearts of people today.

SELFISHNESS

What they were saying in essence was, "Look, this just doesn't work for us. You guys might want to go on over to the new land, but we think it's too hard. We're just not willing to sacrifice. We're staying here, and if that doesn't work for you, well, tough!"

J. Oswald Chambers defines selfishness as: "that which gives me pleasure without considering Jesus Christ's interests." I think the key word in that definition is *pleasure*. As infants our security blanket was usually close by for comfort. Unhappiness could be easily quelled by sucking our thumb. It was easy and instant gratification. Growing up we look for more sophisticated pleasure and security—some of it noble and memorable, some of it we would rather forget. "If it feels good, do it" was a popular phrase before AIDS began to destroy lives. Janet Jackson echoed the attitude of many teens in her song, "What have you done for me lately?" Porno movie shops are often referred to as "pleasure houses." Magazines offer hints on what to do when you *need sex to satisfy* lust. And the number-one reason for divorce today—"I just wasn't happy." We have become a generation ruled by our lusts and passions.

Selfishness has also been defined as prostitution of the God-given capacity to love. Jesus summed up the foundational principles of life with two basic precepts:

> "You shall love the LORD your God with all your heart, with all your soul, and with all your mind." This is the first and great commandment. And the second is like it: "You shall love your neighbor as yourself. On these two commandments hang all the Law and the Prophets."
>
> Matthew 22:37–40

This type of love gives birth to an unconquered goodwill. Bitterness is banished and the consistent hope is for the good of others. This is not man's natural reaction; often it is a victory of the will, a decision of the heart. The selfish person's object is to push others out of the way; the goal of the Christ-centered person is to enable others to climb higher. As long as self is on the throne of your heart, you risk collision with others and failure as a person.

Refusing to allow personal advantage to govern the course of one's life is the first step to conquering selfishness. Nationally known motivational speaker, Zig Ziglar, my good friend, firmly believes "you become a success when you help others to become a success."

SELF-IMAGE

The spies looking at the Promised Land talked more about themselves than they did about the land. "We're grasshoppers! We're small, powerless, hopeless!" They simply did not believe in themselves at all. The giant of a poor self-image stands blocking the path to success with outstretched arms. Throughout the day a taunt roars in your mind: "You'll never make it. You won't be accepted. Just who do you think you are anyway?"

At the risk of being caught talking to yourself, shout back to the giant, "I am a child of the Living God, Creator of heaven and earth. And don't you forget it!"

Gospel singer Ethel Waters was conceived as the result of rape. Her unmarried, teenage mother believed God had a plan for the baby and vowed to keep her. Feeling inferior many years of her life, she later understood God's love for her and for years sang as the featured soloist for Billy Graham crusades. Ethel became famous for her motto: "I know I'm somebody 'cause God don't make no junk!" As my good friend Roland Lundy always says, "I heard that! I know that's right!"

> So God created man in His own image; in the
> image of God He created him; male and female
> He created them.
>
> Genesis 1:27

How can we even dare think poorly of ourselves when we have been created in His very image and by His own hands! That alone is God's standard for the basis of your self-esteem, and there is none higher. The problem of self-image is not a new one. It was evident thousands of years ago, and it still rules many today. In 1910, *Success* magazine editor Orison Swett Marden spoke of believing in yourself: "Self-deprecation is a crime. The great trouble with many of us is that we do not believe enough in ourselves. We do not realize our power. Man was made to hold up his head and carry himself like a conqueror, not like a slave—as a success, not as a failure—to assert his God-given birthright."

Fully understanding the origin of our worth is the foundation of a commitment to excellence. This basis for self-image also serves as a constant factor when circumstances disappoint us. A self-image built on goals and accomplishments will topple with every shift of opportunity. Your source of value is in your creation by God in His image. *Nothing less!*

Look, if you don't believe in yourself, how can you expect others to? Dennis the Menace gave his friend Joey some of the best advice I've ever heard: "Joey, always be good to yourself. Sometimes you're all you've got!"

The saddest thing about a negative attitude is not its destruction to the individual, but its contagious effect on others. The grasshopper syndrome of the eleven men soon infected the entire congregation. A strange thing about it is that both the negative and the positive report required an act of faith. It's all in your decision. What do you want to believe? Notice: "Then all the congregation lifted up their voices and cried." Like a plague it traveled from person to person, destroying hope and leaving weakness in its path.

The majority loudly determined to go against any positive actions. They criticized the motives of the leadership. What do you think you would have done? You may face this type of situation often in your own life. Any time a leader stands up against the flow of the crowd, he or she can expect criticism. Joshua and Caleb faced the task of inspiring the other spies to change from followers to leaders, from whiners to winners, from "I can't" to "I must."

The picture we see in this account is of men who *began* as faithful, but whose faith evaporated in the heat of fear. They magnified the difficulties until their only recourse was to discard all self-image in favor of despair. Instead of operating on the truth, they believed a mirage of what they thought was or even what *might* be.

It's true there were giants in the land, but to the spies they appeared larger and more fierce because their vision was altered by pessimism. They left God completely out of the picture and never even mentioned His name. Joshua and Caleb looked at the giants, but through eyeglasses of faith in God's power and particularly in His will for Israel. While the others shrank in their own sight to grasshoppers, the young leaders stood tall in conviction and trust.

If Joshua and Caleb were teaching a seminar in leadership today, I believe their syllabus outline would include:

1. Don't give in to the fear of the moment.
2. Depend on the resources available in God and not in yourself.
3. Believe in yourself; believe in His will for you.
4. Adjust your vision with the eyeglasses of faith.
5. Always give a good report.
6. Stand against the crowd when you know your conviction is based on faith and truth.

Notice the faith and outlook of the two with a "different spirit." Joshua and Caleb gave a "good report." When the majority said, "No way," they replied, "Way!" In later years, Caleb told his descendants, "I brought back word to him (Moses) as it was *in my heart*" (Josh. 14:7, emphasis mine).

The terms FOCUSED, FAITHFUL, and FINISHERS describe the leadership traits of Joshua and Caleb. These three important attributes will also empower your private and professional life if you adopt them with fervor.

FOCUSED

They were *focused* on the Lord and His power. They never lost sight of their miraculous deliverance from Egypt and the Red Sea. Their vision was clear and unobstructed by opinion. By clearly focusing on the goal, you will find yourself able to see further than those around you see. Cultivate the habit of looking for solutions, opportunities, possibilities rather than obstacles, excuses, and problems. In most situations, you see whatever it is you are expecting to see. Clear vision assures you of sure victory.

> *If a man advances confidently in the direction of his
> dream and endeavors to live life as he imagined it,
> he will meet with success unexpected by most.*
>
>   Henry David Thoreau

FAITHFUL

They were *faithful* to their convictions. I remember my pastor,
Dr. Jack Graham, giving this simple standard for any decision
in life: "It's never right to do wrong, and it's never wrong to do
right." Each of us must remain faithful to the Word of God and
its command to "walk by faith and not by sight." We cannot be
swayed by those who are the loudest or attract the most votes.
We cannot be manipulated by the multitudes. The Chinese have
a proverb: "Noisy on the outside; empty on the inside."

These two young men remained faithful to God even
when the mob attempted to stone them to death (Num. 14:10).
God chose to reward these men of "a different spirit" because
they were faithful to stand alone (14:24). In fact, Joshua and
Caleb were the only two of that generation who were allowed
to enter the Promised Land.

Notice that God did not comment on education, I.Q., ability, or family background, but only on faithfulness. I like what
Mary Kay Ash, founder and president of Mary Kay Cosmetics,
says about ability: "God is not interested in our ability. It is our
availability that He wants."

FINISHERS

Finally, Joshua and Caleb were *finishers*. This positive attitude of faith was a lifelong decision. At the ripe old age of 85,
Caleb thundered "Give me that mountain!" Still standing on

faith in God's power, he claimed the very mountain where the giants lived.

Joshua became the great leader of the nation of Israel. His last address to Israel confirms he finished the race with the same commitment and courage with which he began it:

> Now therefore, fear the LORD, serve Him in sincerity and in truth, and put away the gods which your fathers served on the other side of the River and in Egypt. Serve the LORD! And if it seems evil to you to serve the LORD, choose for yourselves this day whom you will serve, whether the gods which your fathers served that were on the other side of the River, or the gods of the Amorites, in whose land you dwell. But as for me and my house, we will serve the LORD.
>
> Joshua 24:14–15

Desire gives birth to dreams.
Dreams give life to drive.
Drive dares us to DO!

To be a leader is to impact those around us on a daily basis. If you are wondering how effective your leadership can be, use this simple formula. Multiply the length of your own vision times the width of your commitment times the height of your conviction. The result is the volume of your influence.

14

POSSESS YOUR POTENTIAL

Those incredible success stories in periodicals like *Success* magazine just amaze me. I can't help but wonder, "What have they got that I haven't got?" I mean, how did they start with an idea and turn it into millions? Maybe you also have some great ideas. You know you want the Promised Land, but you just don't know how to get there!

The future at times seems as unknown as the galaxies of space. We may not know what the future holds, but we can be sure of *who* holds the future. Look with me now in Deuteronomy 1:2. Moses is leading the children of Israel on an eleven-day journey, but two verses and forty years later, they are all still wandering in the desert. Maybe Moses was too stubborn to stop for directions! But then again, there wasn't a Nomad's Quick Stop or a camel watering station. And anyway, what would he ask? "Hey, do you know where the Promised Land is? God told me it was this way."

For forty years the children of Israel dreamed about and looked for the Promised Land, but they did not possess it. Along the way, there were lots of dry holes, dead ends, and sandstorms.

Joshua was Moses' right hand and served in the background for years. All along, even though Joshua was never aware of it, the Lord was preparing him to lead in the possession of the Promised Land. A review of Joshua's resume shows the one human quality God is looking for in a leader: the consistent offering of a *willing heart*.

> *God prepares us for new opportunities*
> *through everyday experiences.*

Just when it finally looked like trees ahead, the leader, Moses, died, and Joshua was called to step in: "The LORD spoke to Joshua . . . saying, 'Moses my servant is dead. Now therefore arise, go over this Jordan, you and all this people, to the land which I am giving to them'" (Josh. 1:1–2).

Notice that the Lord spoke personally and specifically to Joshua. Do you ever wish you could *hear* the Lord speak? While I have never heard the Lord speak audibly, there have been times His voice has been as clear to me as it was for Moses and Joshua.

God speaks to us today through:

1. *The Word of God* as we read and hear it taught and preached. His truths are evident and His way is clearly written.

2. *In prayer* by listening with our heart. The more we pray, the more we understand His moving in our lives.

3. *Circumstance and opportunity.* Faithfulness on our part leads us into open doors and the security of a chosen future.

4. *The words and advice of consistently godly people.* Always compare counsel with the Word of God.

God's will and way will never be contrary to His Word no matter how much sense the advice seems to make.

At first reading, Joshua's assignment appears to be a fairly simple one; but look a little closer: Joshua's task included taking 600,000 men, women, and children over the Jordan. Difficult, yes, but not impossible. Oh . . . did I mention the river was flooding at the time and the enemy was waiting on the other side? No problem, mon. Bring out the boats.

Guess again. No boats. Just the command of God—"Go." Before Joshua could be crowned as the new leader, he had one small test to pass. You see, there was never any doubt on the Lord's part about the provisions and ability to cross. The only missing factor was Joshua's decision to go forward by faith.

> *A test for us is an opportunity for the Lord.*

The flooding river represents those obstacles in life that hinder us from possessing the potential God has for us. What flood are you trying to cross over? It might be a flood of fear, worry, burnout, failure, depression, anger, bitterness, procrastination, guilt of the past, wrong priorities, contentment with second best, or temptations. In Brazil, a particularly treacherous river was named the "River of Doubt" because of the difficulty encountered in attempting passage. All of us face a strong current of difficulties or apprehension at one time or another.

Maybe you're more worried about the enemy waiting on the other side. This includes:

- Difficult people you must deal with
- A poor self-image
- Spiritual warfare

Remember this, graduate, whenever God gives a *command*, He enables you with a *promise*. While Joshua was still fretting over how to do it, God assured Him it was already accomplished: "Every place that the sole of your foot will tread upon I have given you" (Josh. 1:3).

When we start to count our resources, it's essential to redirect our thinking from *what* we have to *whom* we have. Not only is our promise an abundant one, it comes with a guarantee—the promise of success from the hand of God. "As I was with Moses, so I will be with you. *I will not leave you nor forsake you*" (Josh. 1:5).

If we believe God's promise is before us, His presence beside us, and His power behind us, we shall be willing, ready and able to cross over the flood and meet the enemies waiting on the opposite bank. My daughter has a small poster in her school locker to remind her "if God is for us, who can be against us?" (Rom. 8:31). There is simply no obstacle too great for His power.

So far, we have focused on the promise from God, but now I want us to notice the requirement on Joshua's part: "Only be strong and very courageous, that you may observe to do according to all the law which Moses My servant commanded you; do not turn from it to the right hand or to the left, that you may prosper wherever you go" (Josh. 1:7).

Your part is to:

1. *Be strong and very courageous.* We are commanded to be strong. Weakness is sin because it is devoid of faith.

2. *Obey the commandments of God.* Strength and courage are a result of obeying the laws of God.

3. *Stay true to the Word of God.* We are not to add to the principles of God's Word or to take away—"turn not from it to the right hand or to the left." This means that the law of God is not adjustable to our circumstances; instead the circumstances are to be evaluated against the truths of the Lord's Word.

Courage and obedience are inseparable, and the result is victory—"that you may prosper wherever you go." Joshua believed it. His response in verse 10 is a bold declaration of faith: "Prepare . . . yourselves, for within three days you will cross over this Jordan, to go in to possess the land which the LORD your God is giving you to possess" (Josh. 1:11).

Joshua gave the children of Israel marching orders (Josh. 1:10–16). He told them to:

1. *Get ready* (v. 10). In his case, the preparation was food for the physical body. In our case, the preparation may be physical strength, emotional health, spiritual cleansing, or all of the above.

2. *Remember the promise* (v. 13). Whenever I feel uneasy about the future, I rehearse the wonderful workings of God so far in my life. As the song says, "He didn't bring us this far to leave us." I firmly believe . . .

   > There is great strength in rehearsing
   > what God has already done.

   Rehearsing over and over in my mind the problem and God's answer or the unexpected blessing from His hand, I am strengthened and encouraged to go forward by faith.

3. *Decide to cross over.* The children of Israel responded in verse 16 saying, "All that you command us we will do" (v. 16). You see, obeying God is a decision. It is a choice you must make. The difference between the average person and achiever may not be the circumstances, but how he or she *handles and responds to* the circumstances.

Writer George Bernard Shaw observed, "People are always blaming their circumstances for what they are. I don't believe in circumstances. The people who get on in the world are the people who get up and look for the circumstances they want, and if they can't find them, make them."

Whoomp—there it is! Quit worrying about it, agonizing over it, or speculating the worst. Just cross over the circumstances, possess your potential, and enter the Promised Land.

15

INDECENT PROPOSALS

Indecent Proposal—what an intriguing title for a movie! Perhaps you remember the instant controversy caused by the premise of accepting an indecent proposal in exchange for a million dollars. In this case, an extremely wealthy man sees a woman he wants to have sex with. She turns out to be married, and he makes the husband an offer of one million dollars for one night of sex with his wife. The complications that followed proved that no amount of money is worthy of compromise in values.

Every radio and television talk show debated the question with their guests and audience as America exchanged opinions. Just how much money would be enough to justify saying yes to such an offer?

The question is not worthy of consideration for those of us who have committed ourselves fully to Christ and the principles of God's Word. Any proposal that asks you to trade mere money for an intimate relationship with the holy God is an indecent one. It is an indecent proposal to conclude that God's power is too small to provide satisfaction and peace without giving in to sensual appetites.

While being "on your own" may afford more freedom, it also presents additional pressures to excel according to your own expectations or those others have set for you, conform in order to gain acceptance in a new social setting of friends and peers, and give in to the lure of temptation over what your parents called "forbidden fruit." You will never notice in Scripture a reference to any sin becoming acceptable once you reach a certain age. Sin is sin regardless.

Once they escape the constant watch of their parents, many adolescents rush to try alcohol and/or drugs. Mostly out of curiosity, but sometimes because of peer pressure, the graduate tries the substances "just this once." An incredibly strong enticement causes many to go against all they have believed in and stood for. For millions of alcoholics, "just once" was one time too many.

And before we go any further, let's set the record straight. Alcohol *is* a drug. The legal label does not change its potency. Beware of "new" or "designer" drugs. Their names may be changed, but their damaging effects will remain forever the same. Mind- and mood-altering drugs have been destroying young people for ages.

The Bible repeatedly warns of the dangers of alcohol and drug use:

> Who has woe?
> Who has sorrow?
> Who has contentions?
> Who has complaints?
> Who has wounds without cause?
> Who has redness of eyes?
> Those who linger long at the wine,
> Those who go in search of mixed wine.
> Do not look on the wine when it is red,
> When it sparkles in the cup,
> When it swirls around smoothly;
> At the last it bites like a serpent,
> And stings like a viper.

Your eyes will see strange things,
And your heart will utter perverse things.

Proverbs 23:29–33

Television commercials for alcohol glitter with promises of fun and popularity, but God says "Don't even look on it." The visual temptation is alluring to the mind. Like the cunning of a poisonous serpent, the venom enters through a small bite, but soon affects all senses. Drunkenness affects the language, the will, and decisions of the heart.

Alcohol is listed in statistics as a leading cause of rape, murder, incest, suicide, divorce, and abuse. An overwhelming majority of those in prison today are there because of a crime committed while under the influence of a chemical substance. Of those, half do not even remember committing the offense.

---

*Drunkenness has killed more men than
all of history's wars.*

General John J. Pershing

*To put alcohol in the body is like putting sand
on the bearings of an engine.*

Thomas Edison

Drunkenness finds itself in the company of adultery, murder, homosexuality, and idolatry in several lists of sin (See Romans 13:13; 1 Corinthians 6:9–10; Galatians 5:19–21, 1 Peter 4:3). Many justify the use of alcohol or drugs as a way to deal with emotional pain. In the end their use will only breed more distress: "When shall I awake, that I may seek another drink?"

Your decision on going along with the gang (many of whom will be Christians) on drinking alcohol should be based on scriptural principles rather than feelings or popular opinion:

1. Forego anything that causes others to stumble (1 Cor. 8–10, Rom. 14–15).

2. "Present your bodies a living sacrifice, holy, acceptable to God, which is your reasonable service" (Rom. 12:1b).

3. "And do not be drunk with wine . . . but be filled with the Spirit" (Eph. 5:18). This is an imperative command in the present tense indicating today and every day.

If you already have a drinking problem, put aside the guilt and embarrassment in order to seek immediate help. This habit has the sure grip of a vise, and you will probably need outside help in breaking loose. It *can* be done through the power of Christ. I know this is true because I did it!

Another pressure that will intensify in college is sexual temptation. Try reading a magazine, watching a TV show, or turning on the radio without a reference of some type to sex. It's just about impossible to do. Everywhere your eyes look and in most of the things your ears hear, sexual promiscuity is glorified.

PG and PG-13 movies avoid total nudity but present plenty of sexual activity complete with groans and intensity. Some R-rated movies could be used as sex-instruction videos! What has been labeled "family television" is riddled with sexual language and innuendoes, some of which can be embarrassing if you happen to be watching with a friend of the opposite sex. Even commercials are getting in on the act.

One blue jean ad asked, "Have you ever seen your parents naked?" Perfume commercials are particularly heavy in sensual sell. Even coffee is sold over the suggestion of an affair. Toothpaste is portrayed more often as a tool for dating than it is for prevention of tooth decay. Sometimes after a commercial I am left wondering, "What exactly were they selling?"

Sensuality, homosexuality, fornication, and extramarital affairs confront us at every turn, even when we are not consciously aware of it. The goal is to portray these sexual activities as normal in an effort to reduce guilt. DON'T FALL FOR IT! The Bible gives *specific* rules regarding sex. God created it as a special gift to be enjoyed intimately and privately by husband and wife.

At this stage of life, you will begin to think of dating in terms of approaching marriage. For this reason, the sexual drive will be stronger than ever. There are seven lists of evil in the New Testament. Six of these list fornication at the top, and in the seventh it is second. The primary reason to abstain from sex before marriage is because it is sin, and secondly because it affects your testimony as a Christian.

The wisdom of God's command to wait until marriage has never been more evident than it is in today's society of sexual freedom.

When you consent to sex with a person, you are actually consenting to sex with everyone else he or she has ever been intimate with. I recently read a letter to an advice column from a faithful wife who had been married to the same man for ten years. She came to the marriage a virgin; he was not a virgin at the time of marriage, but claimed to have had only one other sexual partner before her. Both were faithful throughout the marriage. She wanted to know how after ten years of marriage a sexually transmitted disease could suddenly surface and invade her body, particularly since her husband showed no signs of the disease.

The columnist checked the response with a physician before giving this reply: "Sexually transmitted diseases can lie dormant in the body for an indefinite period of time before becoming evident. Your husband can be a carrier and pass it on to you without ever knowing he has it or experiencing symptoms."

There can also be an incubation period with the AIDS virus of sometimes several years before symptoms appear. This is a frightening prospect when you consider the attack on the body's immune system by AIDS (Acquired Immune Deficiency Syndrome). By the time you find out, it can be fatal.

Sexually transmitted diseases (STDs) are highly contagious and can be passed from one person to another through the mouth or genital areas depending on the type and severity of the disease. We hear volumes about AIDS, but little about the fact that there are more than thirty other STDs. Of those, several have no medical cure. Don't be fooled by the flurry of condom popularity. They are not foolproof; only abstinence is.

But you're in love, you say, and plan to marry soon. I tell with tears of the many pregnant young ladies I have counseled who once wore an engagement ring. We have no guarantee of tomorrow. Many an engagement has been broken, sometimes months before the wedding, others on the day of the wedding. A number of factors can interfere in a courtship planned for marriage. Death is always a possibility. Travel, military service, and education are others. The years between thirteen and twenty-one are those in which ideals, habits, and interests are changing. At any time during the dating relationship your feelings may change. If you have already committed the sexual act together, then you enter the next relationship with emotional scars and guilt.

Until you say "I do," continue saying "I won't."

If you truly are in love, you will want to enjoy getting to know each other emotionally and spiritually *before* you know each other physically. Once sexual activity has begun, it overwhelms every other part of the relationship. As a result, couples come to the marriage as strangers. They never really noticed annoying habits or thoroughly discussed ideals and ethics. Sexual pleasure can be strong enough to mask and overshadow basic and incompatible differences in your personalities.

We are warned in 1 Corinthians 6:18 to "flee sexual immorality," literally to run away quickly. Don't flirt with the idea; carefully consider the character of the persons you date. If you find yourself attracted to unspiritual or immoral friends, you have a definite problem of the heart. Stop dating at all until you can receive counseling, because once you have given up control of the sex drive, you open yourself up to more and stronger temptation.

Couples who have sex before marriage have a greater risk of one or both being involved in an extramarital affair. The result is a lack of respect and restraint.

> John has a new way of looking at life. He's tired of his job, his kids, and his wife. He says the secret to his success was in leaving and finding himself. Now he's someone to somebody else.
>
> From "Living Life Upside Down"

If you're considering living together first, you should read these statistics from *New Woman* magazine: "only 26 percent of the women surveyed—and a scant 19 percent of the men—married the person with whom they were cohabiting." Instead of a 50 percent divorce rate for cohabiting couples, it is 75 percent. The odds are three to one against you. So you see, it works just the opposite of what you would assume.

Sexual freedom between men and women is just one of society's affronts on moral excellence. The gay community has as its agenda national and worldwide acceptance of the homosexual lifestyle as normal. I read very recently in a *People* magazine gossip column of two young actresses who had given up their boyfriends to move in together as lovers. Gay parades are given considerable media coverage. Many government officials and leaders are openly proclaiming their gay lifestyle, and court cases for same sex marriages are becoming commonplace.

How should the acceptance by society of the homosexual lifestyle affect your belief? Not one bit, because God's Word does not rise and fall on popularity. Nowhere in the Bible is homosexuality permitted. It is, however, condemned in many places. God hates the sin, but remains faithful in His love of the sinner.

This perversion has not caught the Lord by surprise. It has been going on since ancient days. Always, when mentioned in

Scripture, homosexuality is followed by judgment and condemnation from God.

The most familiar story in the Bible dealing with homosexuality is that of Sodom and Gomorrah (Genesis 18 and 19). We are
told God could no longer stand the wickedness of these cities
and planned to destroy them. Abraham begged God to save
Sodom for the sake of a few righteous people, including his
relatives. God promised to send angels to investigate, and when
they arrived, they were met by homosexual demands. It was
then that God completely destroyed the cities in judgment.

God clearly warns in Leviticus 18:22, "You shall not lie
with a male as with a woman. It is an abomination." To "lie"
with someone, in the Old Testament meaning, indicates the
sexual act. In the New Testament, several passages also apply.
In Romans 1:24–28, the following terms are used in connection
with homosexuality: verse 24—uncleanness, lusts, dishonor;
verse 26—vile passions, against nature; verse 27—shameful,
error; verse 28—debased mind, not fitting. These verses alone
are evidence enough of God's attitude toward homosexuality,
but there are many others.

There are people who will distort these verses and tell you
they interpret the words differently. Do not believe them. The
Word of God speaks clearly and does not need to be indepen-
dently interpreted. In every situation, allow the Word of God
to interpret itself by comparing it with other verses about the
same subject. There is no contradiction of teaching in the Bible.

If you are struggling with homosexuality, please understand
that although God condemns the sin, He still loves you and wants
to help you overcome this lifestyle. The Bible speaks of those
who commit sexual sin as being unable to inherit heaven (1
Cor. 6:9–10), yet tells in the next verse, "Such *were* some of you.
But you were washed, . . . sanctified, . . . justified in the
name of our Lord Jesus and by the Spirit of our God." Healing
and forgiveness are available in Christ. Seek godly counsel for
help in this matter.

What you must decide, *before* you find yourself surrounded by the current of feelings over values, is that you absolutely will not deter from the goal of moral excellence. Without an air of superiority, allow your decision to be public knowledge among your circle of friends. This in itself will relieve you of a tremendous amount of tension. You never know who among your group is struggling with sexual pressure. Your steadfast testimony can be a source of strength to all who know you.

You'll not only be respected, you'll be pleasing to God.

16

Avoid Self-Sabotage

Modern psychology has as its tenant the belief that most of our problems are the result of others' behavior toward us at some particular time in our lives. Sometimes that is true, but very often we have sabotaged ourselves through our own actions. Two decades ago Walt Kelly's precocious cartoon character Pogo instructed us, "We have met the enemy, and he is us."

Ring magazine reported on one Golden Glove Champion fight that was over before it even began. The contender, intent on psyching himself into a fighting mood, punched himself in the face several times. The first self-inflicted blow cracked his jaw; the second broke his nose and rendered him unconscious. He was carried away on a stretcher before his opponent stepped into the ring. All of us have the capacity to sabotage ourselves.

Sabotage has as its root the French word *sabot,* having to do with shoes. During the French Revolution, peasants banged their wooden clogs against iron bars to disrupt a political speaker or civic meeting. They also threw their sabots into the mills to destroy the machinery and bring the work to a grinding halt; thus, the term *sabotage,* means "to destroy" or "stop."

One famous account of this destructive behavior is found in the story of the Prodigal Son in Luke 15:11–32. Tired of his father's rules and restraints, the youngest son ran off to a "far country" in search of freedom to live his own way. We read of no conflict or abuse. This was a selfish young man who took the money and ran, only to waste "his possessions with prodigal living."

No more curfews, deadlines, or responsibilities. He wanted to party-hardy. Some things never change; promiscuity, drunkenness, and drug use are as rampant today as they have ever been. Throughout history the message has been ignored: sin fascinates, then assassinates. Thrills, then kills. Enjoys, then destroys. The very term *prodigal* is translated "addicted to wastefulness." This addiction turns a once-cheerful student into a helpless fool. "I can't help it. I'm so weak. I don't know why I keep doing this" are all phrases spoken by the prodigal.

The search for freedom cost him everything. In fact, in verse 15, he voluntarily gave up his freedom to "join himself" to a pig farmer. The honorable responsibilities and comforts of home were replaced by a job feeding pigs with leftover pig slop for food. To a young Jewish boy who considered pigs to be untouchable, eating their food was the lowest of the low.

Seventies rock star Janis Joplin used to sing, "Freedom's just another word for nothing left to lose." The prodigal had finally found freedom by Joplin's definition. With a wounded will and a punctured pride, he finally "came to himself." The folly of his actions overwhelmed him, and his next thought was to go home.

Oh, how I wish reading this story could keep teens from wasting their lives. For some reason, youth must experience the destruction firsthand before understanding the significance of boundaries, responsibilities, and right living. In this story, the father's forgiveness and love represents that of our heavenly Father to us. Imagine how forgiveness and acceptance felt to this emotionally starved man as he made his way into the open arms of his father. It reminds me of words from the old church hymn, "Come home, come home, ye who are weary, come home." You can *always* come home to the things of God and His love—no matter what. We speak excitedly of physical healings, but there is no greater miracle than a holy God's willingness to freely forgive.

The greatest need of man was met in the death and resurrection of Christ. The greatest price was paid as He gave His life for the atonement of sin and offers the greatest blessing of forgiveness.

Every day I realize more and more the impact of attitude on a life. It is more important than who your parents are, how much money, education, or skills you possess, your appearance, or even your health. Attitude can make or break a relationship, a career, a hereafter.

> *The greatest discovery made in my generation is that a human being can better his life by altering the attitudes of his mind.*
>
> William James

That we have been given the capacity to daily choose our attitude is remarkable to me. The past and the inevitable future cannot be altered; the only winning card we can play is our attitude. Most of the time, it's all we need.

SIGNALS OF SELF-SABOTAGE

In the intensity of the moment, the boxer in our story was unaware of his self-sabotage. You and I, however, can watch for signals of self-defeat.

The first destructive signal is the failure to accept responsibility for the direction of your own life. The blame-game originated in the Garden of Eden when Adam told the Lord it was the fault of "the woman You gave me." He blamed both

God and his wife for his poor choice. Then Eve blamed the serpent, who hissed in laughter because he'd won.

On a sports team, in the office, in a relationship, all parties involved must take ownership for decisions and their consequences. When you blame others, you voluntarily hand over control of your life. By cultivating the ability to accept responsibility for your station in life, careful consideration is given to the thoughts, choices, and dreams of today that will ultimately carry you into tomorrow.

> *No individual raindrop considers itself responsible for the flood!*

The second signal is the self-defeating trait of a lack of people skills. A major consideration for future employment is the ability to get along with people. One Stanford University study listed people skills as responsible for 87 percent of the essential ability to getting hired and staying employed. Product knowledge and experience accounted for only 13 percent of hiring incentives. Clearly, employers would rather spend money and time training than dealing with inner-office conflict. A winning attitude and "can-do" spirit are worth their weight in gold to a company.

Mary Kay Ash built her company from the ground up by believing "every person has an invisible sign hanging from the neck that says, 'Make me feel important.'" Never forget that message when working with others.

The third warning sign of imminent self-sabotage is double-mindedness. James pronounces the double-minded thinker as "unstable in all his ways" (James 1:8). The Greek language paints a word picture of a powerful wind tossing the ocean waves from one direction to the other at will. The waves, though powerful, have no control over whether they will bestow safety or destruction to a ship in their path. Lack of focus breeds scattered thoughts and certain death to goals. Progress is unattainable with double-minded thinking.

If you are having difficulty being taken serious on the job, at school, or by family and friends, perhaps it is because they have watched your intentions being blown about like a scrap of paper on a windy street. Like a small bird caught in a big wind, there is never any surety of where you will end up.

Don't fall into the habit of making halfhearted or partially thought-out decisions. Pursue worthy and noble goals as you think ahead: "What would happen if . . . ? What would happen next?"

Attending a high school reunion, I was amazed to hear high school friends explain why they never reached their goals. As best as I could understand, someone told them it wasn't a good idea and they believed it. They allowed the voice of negative thinking to become the voice of reasoning.

Trivial Pursuit is a game some people have taken to heart as they run from one small idea to another, saying much but doing little. Long before Toys R Us carried the product, Roman soldiers played the first version. After long, exhausting marches the soldiers of the Roman empire would gather at an inn on the outskirts of Rome. Situated at the intersection of three roadways, it was dubbed Tri Via, meaning three streets. There they drank ale and beer through the night, talking aimlessly. Hence, the term *trivia* was born.

The fourth injurious habit is wasting time. The effort to conserve water should be carried over to conservation of time, a nonrenewable resource. The ability to manage your time comes through organization and priorities. It's never that you don't have the time. It will always be that you have not made or appropriated the time for that which is important, lasting, and life-changing. One of my favorite speakers is Dr. John Maxwell. I listen to his tapes often and remember in particular his statement concerning time management: "Unless you manage yourself effectively, no amount of ability, skill, experience, or knowledge will allow you to be successful."

God has given every person the same 24 hours in a day, seven days in a week. Out of that 168 hours in a week, you will average 37 hours of discretionary time; that is, time when you are not at work, sleeping, eating, in class, etc. In that 37 hours, you have to tend to family responsibilities, church service, errands, etc. These duties will take up 2,000 hours a year and 20,000 in a decade. Still, plenty of hours will be left over. It is up to you to harness these hours into productive teams of accomplishment and learning.

Just one hour a day devoted to Bible study and prayer, one hour devoted to exercise, reading, or skill improvement, can have a profound effect over a lifetime. There is an alternative— watch reruns of "Gilligan's Island" for hours at a time on the couch. You'll find yourself shipwrecked and stranded, too, unless you make definite plans.

Am I saying never relax? Never just hang out? No way! Hanging out is one of my favorite things to do. Just keep this in mind every day:

> LIFE IS 10 PERCENT WHAT HAPPENS
> TO ME AND 90 PERCENT HOW I REACT
> TO WHAT HAPPENS.

Take charge today of emotions and attitudes. You might just have to get out of your own way!

17

THE MOUNT OF TEMPTATION

It has been said that opportunity knocks, but temptation kicks the door in! Because the temptation is so abrupt, we can usually deal with it, but subtle snares entrap us without warning. Victor Murray wrote in 1939, "As we scale the mountain of spiritual excellence, temptation follows us all the way, becoming more refined as our lives become more refined, more subtle as our spiritual sensitiveness is keener." Remember, it is the *little* foxes that steal the grapes and spoil the vines. The big ones are looking for blood.

Without question the most difficult mountain you will be challenged to climb is the mountain of temptation. This one mountain dominates the horizon. It appears to be a range of mountains instead of one. This is best illustrated in the life of Jesus Himself. When you consider that even Jesus had to weather this mountain, so will you. I know it is the nineties but it is time to dust off the doctrine of the devil as to ascertain his *modus operandi*. The strategy has remained the same from the Garden of Eden to the blinding glitter of the nineties.

Paul warns in 2 Timothy 2:26, "and that they may come to their senses and escape the snare of the devil, having been taken captive by him to do his will." The Scripture also provides us three occasions when the tempter did his thing.

In 1 John 2:16 we are given a concise listing of the what and how: "For all that is in the world—the lust of the flesh, the lust of the eyes, and the pride of life."

LUST OF THE FLESH: Matthew 4:3 gives us a blow-by-blow description. While Jesus was divine, He was also human. It is only natural after forty days and nights of fasting he would be extremely hungry. The devil always comes at the opportune season. The tempter said, "If You are the Son of God, command that these stones become bread." This temptation came from outside. Jesus could have accomplished that in a New York minute but the test was for Him to ignore His Father and take the situation into His own hands. Lust of the flesh could be any sensual appetite—sex, drugs, food, etc.

PRIDE OF LIFE: In verse 5, Jesus is now taken into the holy city and set on the pinnacle of the temple and the devil said to Him, "If You are the Son of God, throw Yourself down. For it is written: 'He shall give His angels charge over you,' and 'In their hands they shall bear you up, lest you dash your foot against a stone'" (vv. 6–7). You ought to be able to relate to this; it is a challenge to your personhood, your pride, to take the easy way out.

LUST OF THE EYES: Matthew 4:8–9—"Again, the devil took Him up on an exceedingly high mountain, and showed Him all the kingdoms of the world and their glory. And he said to Him, 'All these things I will give You if You will fall down and worship me.'" *All these things will be Yours.* The tempter no doubt showed Jesus all that was appealing in the world: the beauty, the power, the sensuality. The temptation also would be to obtain the crown without enduring the cross. It would have been convenient to lower convictions for the pleasure of the moment.

We see the exact same pattern in the Garden of Eden in Genesis 3:1–7:

> Now the serpent was more cunning than any beast of the field which the LORD God had made. And he said to the woman, "Has God indeed said, You shall not eat of every tree of the garden"? And the woman said to the serpent, "We may eat of the fruit of the trees of the garden; but of the fruit of the tree which is in the midst of the garden, God has said, 'You shall not eat it, nor shall you touch it, lest you die.'" Then the serpent said to the woman, "You will not surely die. For God knows that in the day you eat of it your eyes will be opened, and you will be like God, knowing good and evil." So when the woman saw that the tree was good for food, that it was pleasant to the eyes, and a tree desirable to make one wise, she took of its fruit and ate. She also gave to her husband with her, and he ate. Then the eyes of both of them were opened, and they knew that they were naked; and they sewed fig leaves together and made themselves coverings.

In this passage we see all three temptations:

LUST OF THE FLESH: "When the woman saw it was good for food . . ."

LUST OF THE EYES: "And it was pleasant to the eyes . . ."

PRIDE OF LIFE: "A tree desirable to make you wise . . ." "It will make you as God . . ."

You must recall that each time Satan personalized the plan. He will tailor-make a snare for you. The example Jesus gave us is a sure signal to beware of on every occasion of temptation. Each time He answered Satan in the same way: "It is written." "It is written."

God's Word is our defense. Whatever you do, don't neglect your study of God's Word during the time of transition. The tempter would love to throw you off course during such a critical time when perhaps you will meet your future mate, make a career decision, or if you decide to represent your country as well as yourself in the military, your life could be on the line.

Temptation will come to you when things are going very well and you are content. Adam had just named the animals and he and Eve were enjoying paradise when Satan attacked. Joseph had just been promoted to a better position. David and Solomon were kings of all Israel. Jesus was just beginning His earthly ministry, and all was well. Peter had just walked on water. "Therefore let him who thinks he stands take heed lest he fall" (1 Cor. 10:12).

Temptations may cause me to stumble, but only I can determine if I fall down. This is seen in the life of Joseph.

> *The greater the height, the greater the possibility for a fall, and the greater the damage will be.*

Hebrews 4:14–16 says, "Seeing then that we have a great High Priest who has passed through the heavens, Jesus the Son of God, let us hold fast our confession. For we do not have a High Priest who cannot sympathize with our weaknesses, but was in all points tempted as we are, yet without sin. Let us therefore come boldly to the throne of grace, that we may obtain mercy and find grace to help in time of need."

Don't let such a powerful invitation slip through your fingers. Remember Jesus Christ has been there, too—through the pain and grief, loneliness and betrayal, the fatigue and the hunger, and through the temptation and testing. All of it, but without sin. So walk boldly or run boldly to accept what He is so anxious to give—mercy and strength.

Although you are not alone in your temptations, you do have the final decision. God's power and presence are available.

The question is, will you rely on Him when the urges race within you and the enticements come to you from without?

Jesus realized this when he taught His followers to pray, "and lead me not into temptation but deliver me from evil."

To be all you desire to be, you need to become more and more plugged in to God's Word and His Holy Spirit. Make no provision for the fleshly desires that come from the desire for pleasure, power, and possessions. Dr. William Hendriksen, the author of *New Testament Commentary on the Epistle to the Romans*, portrays these enticements in a most graphic way:

- *Pleasure*—the inordinate craving for the satisfaction of physical appetites.

- *Power*—the lust to shine and to be dominant.

- *Possessions*—the uncontrollable yearnings for material possessions and for the prestige that accompanies them. (You haven't had to climb this mountain of temptation yet, but you will in the days ahead!)

Anyone who meets a testing challenge head-on and manages to stick it out is mighty fortunate. For such persons loyally in love with God, the reward is life and more life. Don't let anyone under pressure to give in to evil say, "God is trying to trip me up." God is impervious to evil and puts evil in no one's way. The temptation to give in to evil comes from us and only us. We have no one to blame but the leering, seducing flareup of our own lust. Lust gets pregnant, and has a baby: sin! Sin grows up to adulthood, and becomes a real killer.

James 1:12–15, *The Message*

How clear an expression of how slippery and treacherous this mountain slope can be.

You are not alone in your struggle: "No temptation has overtaken you except such as is common to man; but God is faithful, who will not allow you to be tempted beyond what you are able, but with the temptation will also make the way of escape, that you may be able to bear it" (1 Cor. 10:13).

There are other temptations that do not present themselves with such clarity of decision; nor are their consequences immediate. Instead they often flow forth to dampen the overall attitude of a person. For example, the temptation to forget how hard you have already worked, how much God loves you, the importance of waiting on God. The temptation to flee or give up, to find fault, or to fail to live up to your God-given potential. Failure is a great robber of the soul's fire, but if you let it be, it can be wonderful teacher of the future.

18

SPACESHIP EARTH

The earth is the Lord's and all its fullness.

Psalm 24:1

The Scriptures, which happen to be the owner's manual on how to keep your spaceship running smoothly, tell us the world was created by His Word (Ps. 33:6 and 148:5) in accordance with His wisdom (Jer. 10:12) and His will (Rev. 4:11).

As stewards of His property, we are responsible for looking out for His interest. Dr. Richard Land, president of the Christian Life Commission of the Southern Baptist Convention, reminds us that mankind's statement of "we come first" is very contradicting to promotions such as "save the whales" and "save the snail darters," and yet support abortion.

Dr. Jack Graham, my good friend and the dynamic pastor of Prestonwood Baptist Church in Dallas, Texas, preached an outstanding sermon on this issue and has graciously allowed me to share the highlights with you.

RESPONSES TO CREATION

How should the Christian respond to the Creator and to the creation that God made? He suggests three ways:

Adoration. Our first response should be adoration. When we look into the telescope and see the majestic galaxies too numerous to count and when we look into the microscope to see a miniature universe, we see the mighty hand of God. This is best illustrated in *The Silent Planet*, written by C. S. Lewis, one of my favorite authors. In his own unique style, he portrays the moon, the sun, and all the stars and planets dancing around the throne of God. There is much music and adoration except for one planet, which has lost its song. It is sick and unable to join the chorus because of its rebellion. But all of creation reflects His glory.

Celebration. Our second response should be to respond to the Creator and creation with celebration. That is why we should enjoy the beauty and diversity of this world. I have been to the top of the Swiss Alps and to 120 feet below sea level, mesmerized by the beauty. The poet Henry Wadsworth Longfellow has colorfully described how nature, "God's oldest testament," speaks for God.

> And Nature, the old nurse, took
> The child upon her knee,
> Saying: "Here is a story book
> Thy Father has written for thee!"
>
> "Come, wander with me," she said,
> "Into regions yet untrod;
> And read what is still unread
> In the manuscripts of God!"

And he wandered away and away
With Nature, the dear old nurse,
Who sang to him night and day
The rhymes of the universe.

Caution. Thirdly, we must approach God's creation with precaution. It is our responsibility to care for this planet, not only as stewards, but for our children and grandchildren. Too often we have abdicated our responsibility to those who deny God.

RESPONSIBILITIES

What in heaven's name is my responsibility? The Christian Life Commission has made available its recommended action steps for information and involvement.

STEP 1: ENDANGERED EARTH

Humans are changing the earth. "The world is warming. Climatic zones are shifting. Glaciers are melting. Sea level is rising. These are not hypothetical events from a science fiction movie. These changes and others are already taking place, and we expect them to accelerate over the next years as the amounts of carbon dioxide, methane and other trace gases accumulating in the atmosphere through human activities increase" (*Scientific American*, April 1989).

"A United Nations-sponsored panel of experts has concluded that worldwide temperatures will rise an unprecedented 2 degrees within 35 years and more than 6 degrees by the end of the next century, if nothing is done to combat global warming. The new forecast . . . predicts that temperatures will be far greater than any experienced in the last 10,000 years" (*Washington Post*, May 26, 1990).

By fouling the air, water and land. "Emissions from fossil fuels—the oil, coal and gas used to produce energy—are creating environmental havoc everywhere. Unprecedented amounts of their toxic byproducts are clogging the atmosphere with pollution, killing the trees and poisoning water with acid rain and—most ominously of all—threatening to warm the globe's climate and change life on this planet forever" (Gannett News Service, December 17, 1989).

"Strong evidence of the effect [of chlorofluorocarbons on the ozone layer] emerged in 1985, when British researchers announced the existence of a seasonal 'hole' in the ozone layer over Antarctica. That was worrisome: ozone between 10 and 30 miles up absorbs the sun's ultraviolet radiation, which has been linked to cataracts, skin cancers and weakened immune systems in humans and other animals, as well as damage to plants" (*Time*, March 13, 1989).

"Researchers have found the first evidence that marine plants in the ocean around Antarctica, the tiny organisms upon which a vast ecosystem depends, are damaged by the ultraviolet light that pours through the seasonal hole in the ozone layer. Laboratory tests at Palmer Station in Antarctica show that ultraviolet radiation can alter the genes of common species of Antarctic phytoplankton, the one-celled marine plants that sustain a food web that includes krill, fish, penguins and whales" (*Washington Post*, July 31, 1990).

"Once inaccessible and pristine, the white continent (of Antarctica) is now threatened by spreading pollution, budding tourism and the world's thirst for oil. . . . The only way to save Antarctica is to convince the countries operating there . . . that it is not worth fouling the only relatively untouched continent left on earth to gain a few extra barrels of oil" (*Time*, January 15, 1990).

Ruining the natural recycling of rain forests. "The world needs trees, lots of them, to store the carbon produced by a growing population that is irreversibly industrialized. The world's forests are like giant utilities, providing an indispensable service to the stability of the planet. Rain forests especially are carbon dumps: trees extract carbon dioxide from the atmosphere, emit the oxygen and store the carbon in their wood, leaves, roots and surrounding soil" (*Newsweek*, December 5, 1988).

"Among the world's untamed and unexplored regions, there is none richer than the Amazon Basin . . . . Scientists say the fires set by ranchers and homesteaders in the Amazon region are spewing into the atmosphere 7% of the carbon dioxide responsible for the global warming process known as the greenhouse effect" (*Time*, April 17, 1989).

"Tropical forests cover some 6% of the world, but they are home for an estimated 60% of the world's species. And they are disappearing at an alarming rate: Some biologists estimate that an area of forest the size of New England is destroyed in the tropics each year" (*U.S. News & World Report*, March 6, 1989).

"Offering what may be the last great hope for saving the rapidly disappearing rain forests, a team of biologists and economists has found that the forest of the Amazon is worth far more money if harvested for fruits and rubber in a sustainable way, than if cut for timber or cleared for cattle ranching" (*Washington Post*, June 29, 1989).

STEP 2: RECYCLING—A CHRISTIAN STEWARDSHIP

The need. Recycling is one way in which every individual, church, business, and community can do something positive to protect and to preserve the earth's environment and to demonstrate good stewardship of the earth's resources.

Recycling is an organized system for collecting, reprocessing, and reusing materials once considered garbage. Every individual in America generates more than 90,000 pounds of garbage over a lifetime. Our nation has run out of places to dispose of the garbage generated by its 250 million inhabitants. From 1978 to 1988 nearly three-fourths (14,000) of the nation's 20,000 landfills closed because they were full. By 1993 an additional 2,000 will close.

Landfills are not the answer to our garbage problem. They contaminate ground water and create methane and other gases harmful to the atmosphere, humans, animals, and plants. Recycling is a viable alternative to burying garbage that can reduce disposable waste by 60 to 80 percent.

The biblical mandate. Aside from the obvious need, when we recycle, we also fulfill a mandate given to the human family of God. According to Genesis 2:15, humans were given work which included tilling and keeping the earth. "To till" the ground implies responsible use of the earth's resources. "To keep" the earth literally means "to guard" and "to protect" it. Our failure in both of these assignments has created a global crisis which threatens the health and well-being of the earth and its inhabitants. Recycling is one positive way to return to the God given role of responsible stewardship of the earth.

How to begin recycling.
   1. Effective recycling begins with precycling. Consider the amount of garbage to be generated before buying a product. Buy products made from recycled material. Purchase items packed in recycled packaging. Reject product brands that are overpackaged. Avoid plastics wherever possible.

   2. Reduce disposable garbage by reusing items at home and at work. Use glasses and mugs instead of paper or Styrofoam cups, rags instead of paper towels, cloth instead of plastic disposable diapers, cloth instead of paper napkins, and so forth. Use of disposable items in most cases is a matter of convenience and not one of necessity. Use of such items greatly contributes to the garbage glut with which our generation as well as future generations must cope. Let us not sacrifice health and well-being for convenience.

   3. Separate recyclables into categories. Secure a container for each category: clear glass, colored glass, aluminum, tin/steel cans, plastics, motor oil, and compostable

garbage. Start a compost outdoors. A compost can include grass clippings, leaves, and biodegradable foodstuffs.

4. Place separated items in a recycling bin. Many communities are beginning some form of recycling program from curbside to community containers. Some supermarkets and other businesses are offering recycling bins on their property to encourage recycling. As the garbage glut increases, more of these will become available.

     Rural homes and communities present the greatest challenge because recycling bins are not as readily available in these areas. Recycled items must be taken to the nearest village or urban collection center.

5. Begin a recycling program in your church or community. Recycling bins are obtainable, often at no charge and can be placed in any community or rural area. Information on the placement of recycling collection facilities should be obtained from your state recycling coordinator. Every state in the nation has a recycling coordinator. If you do not know the name and address of yours, please contact the Christian Life Commission at 615/244-2495 or write to 901 Commerce Street, Suite 550, Nashville, TN 37203-3696.

STEP 3: ENVIRONMENTAL FACTS

- The smallest drip of a leaky faucet can waste over 50 gallons of water per day. Only 3 percent of the world's water is fresh water.

- Reducing your thermostat only one degree reduces your heating bill 2 percent.

- A single house plant can reduce hazardous indoor pollution by up to 67 percent in only 24 hours.

- Composting food and yard waste can reduce garbage by as much as 28 percent.

- By recycling, the average family can save 6 pounds of glass per person, per month.

- Only 20 percent of plastic soda bottles are currently being recycled.

- Only 5 percent of the hazardous waste in homes is taken to one of the 23 existing collection centers in the United States.

- Recycling motor oil prevents soil and water contamination.

- The average person throws out 6 pounds of steel/tin cans per month. These cans can be recycled.

- Aluminum foil, as well as cans can be recycled. Each aluminum can recycled saves 95 percent of the energy needed to produce one new can.

- Plastic bags can be washed, reused and when discarded they can be recycled.

- Buying items in recycled packaging and refusing products that are over-packaged reduces solid waste.

- When replacing appliances, recycle discarded ones through salvage yards or charitable collection centers and shop for energy efficient replacements.

- Energy Miser incandescent light bulbs save energy while long-life bulbs use more energy than standard bulbs.

- Become better educated by reading for ways to be a better steward of our world.

19

ONWARD AND UPWARD

As the traditional strains of "Pomp and Circumstance" filled the air, all your family and friends at graduation waved proudly. It was an exciting occasion for everyone. High school was finally over! For parents and graduates alike, this was a time to rejoice.

As exciting as the evening was, I remember my major goal for the night was to keep my hat positioned on my head long enough to accept my diploma! As the newly graduated class marched out at the conclusion of the event, the school band played. It's ironic that now looking back I don't remember much about what the speaker had to say, but I do vividly recall I got a classic case of *future shock*—you know, that sense of insecurity and disorientation.

It struck me as strange that while my friends and I were celebrating the end of school and the completion of four years of learning, the ceremony was built on encouraging us as we headed for a new beginning in the future. The word *commencement* means "new beginning, fresh start." All the while I was thinking, "Finally, I made it. Now I'll just ease on down the road of life for a while." When I finally listened to the commencement speaker, he was telling me to climb the mountains of life.

Perhaps you have these same heavy thoughts. Alvin Toffler, author of *Future Shock,* predicts that you and your friends "will experience more rapid change than any time in human history!" In fact in his book *Power Shift,* he calls this period of time the hinge of history until the year 2025. But don't feel any pressure . . . yeah, right!

Years later, as I continually study the Scriptures, I see that God is always calling us to higher ground. The Old Testament often refers to God as being at the "high place," and the Lord Himself frequently called His prophets to "come up" in order to commune with Him, receive instruction, and to private, personal worship.

In Numbers 23:3–4, the prophet Balaam went to the high place to meet God, "and God met Balaam." Samuel, the priest of Israel, worshiped and made sacrifice for the people before the Lord at the high place. "Moses went up to God, and the LORD called to him from the mountain" (Exod. 19:3). In Revelation 4:1, God personally called John to "Come up here."

These examples in Scripture paint an awesome picture of a spiritual mountain-climbing experience. There are four mountains in the Scripture that offer us inspiration and insight. We have discussed these throughout the book:

1. The mountain of INSTRUCTION.
2. The mountain of DEDICATION.
3. The mountain of TRANSFORMATION.
4. The mountain of TEMPTATION.

Each of these mountain-climbing stories is suitable for motivating us "above and beyond" to the twenty-first century. Their lessons will continue to guide, encourage, and motivate until the end of time.

MOUNT OF INSTRUCTION

Moses had delivered the people out of bondage and together they looked toward a new beginning and a new life in the Promised Land. If you will allow the play on words, you have now moved "out of bondage" as you graduate and face the Promised Land of Opportunity. With the parting of the Red Sea, Egypt and bondage are left behind and freedom to choose a new future is ahead. (*Your* graduation might even be called a "miracle" by some!) The journey Moses faced was a difficult one, with many suffering, some dying, but also many births, marriages, and joyous celebrations. So it is in our real journey of life.

As Moses led the people, he depended heavily on the direction of God. It is worthy to note that although Moses became a beloved leader—he had wrought miracles, had overcome the powerful Pharaoh of Egypt—his very next step as God's man after the great victory was to seek guidance, advice, and a basis for all truth. As a result, God spoke personally to him with direct instructions in the way he should go, beginning with the Ten Commandments.

One thing you can depend on is that when God speaks it will be clear, sure, and loud. While some live as though these are the "Ten Suggestions," make no mistake that the living and true God said "Ten Commandments" or "Laws." In Exodus 19, Moses went up to the mountain to meet with God and to receive His next instructions. This mountaintop experience was an intense one, and Moses came down from the mountain radiant with the presence of God and changed in his heart.

Unfortunately, he descended from glory into chaos. As God was laying out a plan of blessing for the people, they were having the first "rock concert" down below. Music was blaring as the drunkenness abounded, and the sexual orgies that accompanied much of the idol worship of the day was rampant. What God was teaching Moses on that mountain was much more than a set of laws: He continued instruction in leadership of a people whose memories were short-lived, whose hearts thought only of self, and whose convictions were based on the crowd.

You see, the need for truth and wisdom will never come to an end as long as you have life in your body. With the constant change in technology and the seesaw morals of society, basic unchanging tenets will always be necessary.

However, we need now to distinguish between *instruction,* which is the foundation of life and all that you are, and *education,* which is the gathering of information in order to achieve goals and success in the future. These two combine together to make a total person who continues to grow and excel.

Education is the acquisition and practice of new methodologies, skills, and attitudes. Author Alvin Toffler defines learning as "a process of preparing to deal with new situations." True education is knowing how to learn and how to change as information, research, and technology advance.

This mountain of instruction that Moses climbed also taught him to deal with change: taking what you already know and learning to do it better and more productively. It is learning how and when to say NO and saying YES to what God has for you.

But what you need to understand is that there is one part of your instruction that you must never change; that is, the basic laws laid down by the Lord Himself. Anything that is contrary to what God has written in His Word is wrong, regardless of present sentiment or circumstance. While we gain information and techniques, we must not forget to remain unchanged in the instruction of the Word of God, the Bible. There is a clear-cut pattern to what is right and what is wrong. Learn it, memorize it, keep it in your heart.

Can a book written hundreds and even thousands of years ago still apply to you in this futuristic and complex world? Yes it can, and yes it does. Solomon observed that "there is nothing new under the sun," and indeed, the sins of man have remained the same since creation. They may be packaged differently, presented in a flashier design, seem totally sophisticated or complex, but they are the same sins of the heart that apply to the same laws of God since time began.

If you've ever wondered how you can please God and also be looked up to by people, let me show you God's instruction: "My son, do not forget my law, /But let your heart keep my commands; /For length of days /And long life and peace they will add to you. /Let not mercy and truth forsake you; /Bind them around your neck, /Write them on the tablet of your heart, /And so find favor and high esteem /In the sight of God and man" (Prov. 3:1–4).

While most of us are concerned about being looked down on because we don't live the way the world lives, God tells us that we can be looked up to because of who we are, how we live, and what kind of attitudes we portray to others.

In Hebrew the word *mercy* in the quotation above from Proverbs is *chessed*, meaning loving-kindness; it literally involves and encompasses the whole person. It tells of your attitude toward the needs of others for their body, soul, and mind.

BODY: the relieving of wants and needs. Offer food and clothing, money if necessary, to aid those God puts in your path. Every second of every day, three more babies are born that need to be fed. Ninety percent of these births are in countries where malnourishment is a way of life.

SOUL: the compassion and prayer for salvation and spiritual matters. Ask those around you for their prayer needs, expressing an interest in the things that trouble them. Become known as "one who cares."

MIND: the forgiving of one who wrongs you; the giving of godly counsel and wisdom. Stand tall in the name of the Lord and be ready to give an answer to those who ask you "Why?" "Sanctify the Lord God in your hearts and always be ready to give a defense to everyone who asks you a reason for the hope that is in you" (1 Pet. 3:15).

Coming down from that mountain, I am sure Moses felt both great anger and deep depression. How could they so quickly forget all that God had done, all that Moses had endured? He had two choices at that moment: to join the crown and give in, or to determine in his heart to be more deeply dedicated than ever.

Moses stood before the people with a new countenance, a mission from God; yet his greatest mountain now faced him. You will often find that when things are going the best, when you feel the most organized and focused, a mountain will seemingly appear from nowhere and you then face a choice. You can move from the sure ground of dreams to finish what you start by climbing and conquering the mountain of dedication.

As we embark on a new journey of life, let us adopt the countenance of Moses as he came down from the mountain with the excitement of the God-given mission radiating across his face.

MOUNT OF DEDICATION

This is a mountain that everyone will stand before. As you look back and see the number of times you faced it, you will see how much more important your intensity in climbing this mountain will be in the future. What seemed so big in the last few years—cheerleading, swim team, football, chorus, drama, etc.—will be small compared to the challenges ahead. Look around you; remember how full the room was at the beginning of tryouts? The room on the first day of college will be crowded. Little by little, there will be those who drop out, who give up, who decide they don't want to pay the price.

To *dedicate* is to keep pure and clean that which is destined for sacred use and to consecrate or declare or proclaim that one is set apart seriously for a special purpose. What a definition of a Christian! God has chosen you as a special person with a definite purpose in life.

Gideon, for instance, was a man called by God to a specific task. "And it came to pass, when the children of Israel cried out to the LORD because of the Midianites, that the LORD sent a prophet to the children of Israel" (Judg. 6:7–8). The angel of the Lord then came to Gideon as he was threshing wheat (interesting, isn't it, that God called him to such a special anointing while he was going about his everyday responsibilities?). "Go in this might of yours, and you shall save Israel from the hand of the Midianites. Have I not sent you?" (v. 14). Now Gideon knew who he was and he tried to convince God that He was looking for someone else: "O my Lord, how can I save Israel? Indeed my clan is the weakest in Manasseh, and I am the least in my father's house" (v. 15). God's answer was all that He needed to know—"Surely I will be with you, and you will defeat the Midianites as one man" (v. 16).

Now God took this weak nobody and gave him instructions. By simple obedience Gideon found that he soon had thirty-two thousand men at his side ready to go to battle with him in the name of the Lord. This must have been a tremendous support to his confidence, but in the very next verse God told him, "The people who are with you are too many . . . lest Israel claim glory for itself against Me, saying, 'My own hand has saved me'" (Judg. 7:2).

Two checkpoint tests were set up to send away those who were not fit for the battle. The first was the test of the COWARDLY. When Gideon proclaimed that those who were afraid should depart at once, twenty-two thousand of the people returned home, and ten thousand remained. The interesting thing here is that they didn't take the time to hear out the plan or even be fully appraised of the situation. Instead they were watching a movie in what is called the "theater of the mind." Wild imaginations often overcome us as we take the smallest situation and play it out with a domino effect of all that can go wrong. The Israelites were afraid of their own thoughts! "God has not given us the spirit of fear, but of power and of love and of a sound mind" (2 Tim. 1:7).

The second test was for the CARELESS. They weren't afraid, but they were also not aware of the diligence and caution required to win over the enemy. God told Gideon to take them to the water to drink. Those who lapped from the water as a dog would remain; those who got down on their knees would be sent back. You see those who lapped hand to mouth were always ready, but those who knelt down were too relaxed and could be overtaken by surprise. They did not think through their method and gave no attention to the results of their behavior. They were too secure in themselves.

The final exam was only for the COMMITTED. Now Gideon is left with three hundred men, each with a trumpet, an empty pitcher, and a torch. This doesn't sound like much, does it? Ah, but he also had the sure Word of God and the promise of victory. In fact, God's plan was so innovative that the Israelites never actually had to fight. In fear, the Midianites killed each other. Those who were left fled in terror.

CONCLUSION

Many unprepared graduates will handle the turmoil of tomorrow in the same way: with panic, fear, and hasty decisions. Without the shield of faith and the sword of the spirit, which is the Word of God, the graduate will not see the promise of victory fulfilled. You may have received many graduation gifts. Perhaps this book was one. These gifts were given in shiny paper and tidy packages, but life is not handed to us so neatly and beautifully. Life is a daily process of change. Look out the window! You will see the world is experiencing enormous change and great upheaval. Wars will be fought. Sports teams will win and lose. Political leaders will come and go. Technology will continue to be a double-edged sword, capable of great help or great harm. In this sweeping current of change, you must be steadfast in your goal of excellence. Translated from the Latin, *excellence* is literally "to rise above." This is my personal prayer for your future—that you would commit daily to rise *above* and even beyond . . .

In the Sermon on the Mount, Jesus taught this parable about the wise man and the foolish man:

> Not everyone who says to Me, "Lord, Lord," shall enter the kingdom of heaven, but he who does the will of My Father in heaven. Many will say to Me in that day, "Lord, Lord, have we not prophesied in Your name, cast out demons in Your name, and done many wonders in Your name?" And then I will declare to them, "I never knew you; depart from Me, you who practice lawlessness."
>
> Therefore, whoever hears these sayings of Mine, and does them, I will liken him to a wise man who built his house on the rock: and the rain descended, the floods came, and the winds blew and beat on the house; and it did not fall, for it was founded on the rock. But everyone who hears these sayings of Mine, and does not do them, will be like a foolish man who built his house on the sand: and the rain descended, the floods came, and the winds blew and beat on that house; and it fell. And great was its fall.
>
> Matthew 7:21–27

In addition to the upheaval of the world, you will have to deal with the whirlwind of change happening in your own personal life. You have two options before you: to be white-knuckled with fear or to look wide-eyed at the possibilities. Do not leave home without a personal faith in the living God. I made this life-changing decision as a senior in high school. This faith will enable you to have a firm foundation and empower you to face up to your future with excellence and enthusiasm.